AF655878

This book is a novel offering on a subject that is otherwise perceived as somewhat boring and technical one, and on which so much has already been written. Its presentation in the form of conversations is very imaginative. The book succeeds well not only in demystifying GST but also in piquing interest of people not directly connected with it—housewives, students, buyers of real estate, millennials who shop online, etc. Yet, it does not compromise on its rigour and accuracy. Eminently readable!

Vivek Johri, Principal Chief Commissioner of Customs, Government of India

After reading the book, I must appreciate the commendable task of drafting and presenting the concept of GST in a way that makes it very interesting and easy to understand by a layman. The book explains the need of introducing GST very thoroughly and makes the reader to rethink their negative stance on the subject.

For small businessmen, or people with limited technical knowledge, the book can act as a manual to enter the world of GST and help them guide through wherever they are stuck—how to obtain registration, what taxes need to charge and pay, which return needs to file and many more. Moreover, as far as industries or sectors are concerned, this book has explained and addressed various issues, challenges and impact areas faced by them in a simple and lucid way.

Motilal Oswal, Managing Director and CEO, Motilal Oswal Financial Services Limited

GST for the Layman by Apeksha Solanki is a must-read book for everyone, from entrepreneurs and homemakers to CEOs of leading MNCs. The book highlights, explains and dissects the very basics of GST, a structure that can be confusing and downright daunting for many. Apart from being an effective handbook, the book also assists an individual on the registration process, payment of GST, filing returns, which, according to me, are the USPs of this book. Thank you for this wonderful, informative and interactive read.

Sharlene Batlivala, CEO, Communiqué Public Relations

The book explains the complex concept of GST clearly and accurately that reflects the thoroughness of the research that has gone into bringing out this publication. It is an excellent and reader-friendly book, and I am confident that it will be a great gift to those who buy it. I am sure the book would appeal to a much larger audience, from people within the broad discipline to people who are not from this field.

Mani Kalra Bhasin, PhD, Associate Professor, Department of Education, Lady Irwin College, University of Delhi

A timely book that articulates the concept of GST in a coherent and concise manner. An honest attempt at providing answers to complex questions on GST through relevant examples explained in layman's terms. Overall, an informative read.

Ajay Seth, CFO, Maruti Suzuki India Limited

A must-have for all entrepreneurs. A complicated subject like GST has been explained in a unique manner that is very easy to read and grasp. It adequately covers all important and relevant aspects of the subject.

Manik Malik, CFO, BPTP Limited

GST
FOR THE LAYMAN

GST FOR THE LAYMAN

How It Impacts Your Daily Life

Apeksha Solanki

BLOOMSBURY
NEW DELHI • LONDON • OXFORD • NEW YORK • SYDNEY

BLOOMSBURY INDIA
Bloomsbury Publishing India Pvt. Ltd
Second Floor, LSC Building No. 4, DDA Complex, Pocket C – 6 & 7,
Vasant Kunj, New Delhi 110070

BLOOMSBURY, BLOOMSBURY INDIA and the Diana logo are trademarks of Bloomsbury Publishing Plc

First published in India 2020
This edition published in 2020

Copyright © Apeksha Solanki 2020
Pictures © Apeksha Solanki 2020

Apeksha Solanki has asserted her right under the Indian Copyright Act to be identified as the Author of this work

All rights reserved. No part of this publication may be reproduced or transmitted in any form or by any means, electronic or mechanical, including photocopying, recording or any information storage or retrieval system, without the prior permission in writing from the publishers

Bloomsbury Publishing Plc does not have any control over, or responsibility for, any third-party websites referred to or in this book. All internet addresses given in this book were correct at the time of going to press. The author and publisher regret any inconvenience caused if addresses have changed or sites have ceased to exist, but can accept no responsibility for any such changes

ISBN: PB: 978-93-89812-25-1

2 4 6 8 10 9 7 5 3 1

Typeset in Manipal Technologies Limited
Printed and bound in India by Thomson Press India Ltd.

FSC www.fsc.org MIX Paper from responsible sources FSC® C010615

Bloomsbury Publishing Plc makes every effort to ensure that the papers used in the manufacture of our books are natural, recyclable products made from wood grown in well-managed forests. Our manufacturing processes conform to the environmental regulations of the country of origin

To find out more about our authors and books visit www.bloomsbury.com and sign up for our newsletters
For sale in the Indian subcontinent only

To my anxiety, I finally won you over

. . . well, almost!

CONTENTS

PREFACE

The idea of writing this book was conceived while observing the struggles of people in different walks of life dealing with the newly introduced indirect tax law—Goods and Services Tax (GST)—in the country. The changing landscape of indirect tax laws has sown the seed of doubt in people's mind on the applicability of GST and how it compares to the erstwhile law (primarily, Excise and Service Tax). This book has been written with an intention to help the reader understand the basics of GST law and how it impacts a person's aspects of life, which is the cornerstone of the book. It also tries to bring about awareness amongst readers as to why India decided to overhaul their entire indirect tax system. The book is written with lucidity and in an interactive manner, which would make the subject interesting to read. The book does not delve into the greater technicalities on the subject and is written with the objective of bringing forth the fundamentals of GST that every common man must know.

This is a self-help book on GST which is intended to make the readers aware of the applicability of GST on some of the most regular/important transactions that a person deals with on a daily basis. This would ensure that you are never tripped in the name of GST whenever you go shopping or buy real estate or car or any such thing. The unique feature about this book is the DIY steps to do some of the basic compliances like obtaining GST registrations, payment of GST or filing of returns, etc. Also, some tips are provided to help you make a wise decision in some of the transactions that you may encounter in day-to-day life.

The book is divided into two parts—Part A and Part B. Part A describes the basic GST law and Part B deals with different industries/daily-life situations and how GST would make an impact on the same.

If you are an entrepreneur and worried about GST registrations, we have you covered! You want to start selling goods through your own portal or through various e-commerce portals, we have you covered! We have you covered on applicability of GST on loans, salary, banking transactions, travel, movies, restaurants and much more!

Even though the book covers the elementary aspects of the GST laws, it has been compiled after thorough research and much thought as to cover the most important transactions that a person may come across in everyday life and explained through simple illustrations. Hope you find this book useful.

I would also like to take this opportunity to thank a few people without whom this book would have been difficult to complete. First of all, I would like to thank Nikita for having faith in me to take up this project. I would also like to thank my *karma* for throwing every obstacle possible and yet help me scrape through it. My husband for being so supportive and however clichéd it may sound—last, but not least, my parents for their blessings, without which this piece of work would not have met its rightful end.

PART A

GST AT A GLANCE

An Introduction to GST

Hello, how are you doing?

I am okay, how are you doing?

Very well! You seem to be in some deep thought. May I ask what is bothering you?

You know, it's been two years since GST was introduced and I am still a bit clueless about it. There is still so much buzz and so much happening around it but I don't understand it. Is it really that huge a tax reform as everyone claims it to be? I mean, first, we paid service tax and VAT and now, we pay GST and that too, at a higher rate! Is it even benefiting us?

Oh dear! Of course, GST is a huge reform and it has huge benefits. It is important for everyone in the country to understand it. It has impacted everyone, from a business person to the common man, from students to homemakers. It isn't that complicated after all.

Don't people call you GST Gyani (GG) for the in-depth knowledge you have on the subject? Could you please help me understand GST?

Hahaha! Sure, let's sit down and I'll explain everything to you!

Let me first give you a brief background on GST.

Background of GST

Goods and Services Tax, or, as we more commonly know it, GST, was introduced in India on 1 July 2017. The talks began in the year 2000 during the Atal Bihari Vajpayee government. After a gruelling wait of 17 long years and a period of heated discussions and deliberations, GST finally saw the light of day under the Modi government. GST is a tax levied on supply of goods and services. It is a single tax on supply of goods and services, right from the stage of manufacturer to the stage of ultimate consumer. It has been implemented with the purpose of levying a single indirect tax across the nation, aiming at unifying India as a single unified market.

Umm ... sorry to interrupt, but what is indirect tax?

In India, we have two types of taxes, viz., direct tax and indirect tax.

Direct tax: Direct tax is where the taxpayer is the tax bearer. In other words, the person who is liable to pay tax to the government is the one who is ultimately bearing the tax. The burden of tax cannot be shifted in this case. Like in the case of income tax, the person who pays income tax from their own pocket, is ultimately the same person who is also depositing the tax with the government.

The most common examples of direct tax applicable in India are income tax, the erstwhile wealth tax (which is now abolished), etc.

Indirect tax: Indirect tax is where the taxpayer and the tax bearer are different. In other words, the burden of tax is shifted from the taxpayer to the ultimate consumer. Like in the case of VAT or service tax, the liability to pay tax to the government would rest with the seller of goods or the service provider; however, the ultimate burden of tax was borne by the consumer of such services (i.e. tax was finally paid by the ultimate consumer).

For example, when Mr A takes salon services, he pays service tax to the salon and that service tax is deposited with the government by the salon owner. Which means that even though the cost of service tax is borne by Mr A (tax bearer) the taxpayer is the salon owner.

But these indirect taxes are not levied anymore, right?

That's right. A lot of erstwhile indirect taxes levied by the Central or state governments have been subsumed under GST. under the current GST regime, none of the previous indirect taxes are applicable on goods or services. Just one tax—GST—is applicable for every transaction in goods or services, at every stage in the value chain.

Taxes Subsumed under GST

The following taxes, in Table 1.1, (which were applicable before July 2017) have been subsumed under GST:

TABLE 1.1

	Taxes Subsumed	Purpose of Tax
Taxes Levied by Central Government	Central Excise Duty	Tax on manufacture of goods
	Service Tax	Tax on provision of service
	Additional Duties of Excise	To collect additional excise duty on specified products
	Additional Duties of Customs (CVD)	Tax on imported goods at the rate of excise duty applicable on such goods
	Special Additional Duty of Customs (SAD)	Tax on imported goods at the rate of VAT applicable on such goods
	Central Surcharges and Cesses	Additional tax applicable on some of the duties or taxes mentioned above
Taxes Levied by State Government	Value Added Tax (VAT)	Tax on sale of goods within state
	Central Sales Tax (CST)	Tax on inter-state sale of goods
	Luxury Tax	Tax on luxury products
	Entry Tax	Tax on entry of goods into the state
	Octroi	Tax on entry of goods by the local authorities
	Entertainment and Amusement Tax (except when levied by the local authorities)	Tax on movies/major commercial shows, nightclubs, etc.

»

	Taxes Subsumed	Purpose of Tax
	Purchase Tax	Tax on purchase of specified goods
	Taxes on Advertisements	As the name suggests
	Taxes on Lotteries, Betting and Gambling	As the name suggests
	State Surcharges and Cesses	Additional tax applicable on some of the duties or taxes mentioned above

However, there are a few indirect taxes from the pre-GST era which are applicable even after the introduction of GST.

Taxes Not Subsumed under GST

1. Basic Customs Duty
2. Road and Passenger Tax
3. Toll Tax
4. Property Tax
5. Stamp Duty
6. Electricity Duty

Also, there are a few products which are outside the purview of GST, on which the erstwhile regime of indirect taxes continues to apply:

1. State taxes on alcohol for human consumption.
2. Taxes on manufacture and sale of five specified petroleum products—crude, petrol, diesel, aviation turbine fuel (ATF) and natural gas.
3. Taxes on sale of electricity.

Woah! That's a lot of taxes under one GST! I did not know that we paid so many taxes!

But then, why did we require GST? When we had such a detailed indirect tax regime already in place, why did we have to go through this whole big change? The industry and people had to face so much discomfort because of this!

Need for GST

GST was required for many reasons:

1. *Increased Transparency in Taxes Levied*: GST would help in the transparency of taxes levied on the supply of goods or services. Earlier, different taxes were applicable by the Central government or state governments on the same product. The ultimate consumer did not know what and how many taxes they

were paying for a particular product. Like in the case of excise duty, which was levied on manufacture of goods, the ultimate consumer did not know that the product they were buying also included excise duty, since the only tax applicable at the stage at which they bought the product might have been VAT. under the current regime, since there is just one tax at every stage in the value chain, the consumer knows how much tax they are paying for a particular product or service.

2. *Reduction in Multiplicity of Taxes*: Multiple taxes levied by both sets of governments led to a lot of disputes and unhappy taxpayers. Further, it even discouraged foreign investment in India. A complex tax structure and the difficulty with which a company could begin its business here, were big dampeners when it came to foreign investments. With GST, the complexity of indirect taxes has been reduced to a great extent and made the system more investor-and-taxpayer-friendly.

3. *Seamless Flow of Tax Credits*: GST resolves a major issue of the cascading effect of taxes. In the earlier regime, taxes levied by the

> Central government were not provided as credit for taxes levied by state governments and vice-versa. In this process, such taxes formed part of the cost of the product and led to a situation of tax on tax and an ultimately higher cost to the consumer.

For example, a salon service provider was liable to charge service tax from its customers. However, to provide for such salon services, it had to procure some inputs like scissors, hair spray, hair colours, furniture and air-conditioner. While buying such inputs, the salon would have paid VAT on them. However, since input VAT (i.e. VAT paid on purchase of inputs) cannot be set-off against service tax to be paid on output service (i.e. service tax to be paid on salon service), VAT forms part of cost and output service tax charged from the consumer would be charged on the cost price of inputs plus VAT paid on such inputs. This led to a situation of tax on tax and increased the tax burden of the end consumer.

Under the GST regime, the tax credits are available at every stage, since there is just one tax on all products at every stage in the supply chain throughout the country. Therefore, the problem of tax on tax gets eliminated and there is seamless flow of tax credit throughout the value chain (*the concept of input tax credit is explained in detail in Chapter 3*). In the above example, while buying the inputs, GST would be charged. However, since the GST on input products would now be available as set-off against GST charged on the output services, the input GST will not form part of the cost when charging GST on output services. Hence, the overall tax burden for the ultimate consumer would be reduced, which in effect, reduces the overall price of the service availed.

4. *Reduction in Compliances:* under the pre-GST era, a taxpayer would have to do the following for every tax law applicable to it:
   (a) Take separate registration.
   (b) Pay tax.
   (c) File returns.
   (d) Separate assessments and appeals under each law.

So, if a company manufactures products and has multiple outlets from which it sells its manufactured product, then it would have to follow the above compliances separately for excise law, service tax law, VAT law and any other local taxes and laws that may be applicable to it. Remembering compliance dates and following different rules and procedures under each law was a time-consuming task and a costly affair. However, under the GST regime, all this can be done under the umbrella of just one law—GST Act, 2017—and hence, the hassle to remember so many different laws is reduced. With just one indirect tax applicable, the time, cost and effort of the taxpayers has reduced significantly.

5. *Simplification of Inter-state Movement of Goods*: In the pre-GST era, movement of goods from one state to another was a huge task and involved a lot of time and cost. A lot of administrative formalities were required at both the state and local municipal levels, which caused delay in movement of goods and increased the overall cost of transportation. With the introduction of E-WayBills under GST regime, inter-state movement of goods has become a breeze (*the concept of waybills is explained in detail in Chapter 5)*

6. *No Credit for Central Sales Tax*: under the erstwhile indirect tax regime, the sate governments levied CST on inter-state movement of goods. However, no credit of CST was available to the purchaser of goods

while discharging CST liability on further sale of goods. Hence, the cost of inter-state movement of goods increased, as no credit for tax was available on the same.

I see all the disadvantages under the previous indirect tax regime. But, what will then happen to the state revenue? With all the indirect taxes of the centre and state governments subsumed under GST, how is each government going to have its own share of revenue?

Well, GST is designed in such a manner that each government will have their own share of revenue through the tax collected.

Structure of GST

GST has the following components:

1. For supply of goods and services within the state/union territory, i.e. for intra-state supply, GST would be applicable on each transaction in the following manner:
   (a) Central Goods and Service Tax (CGST), which is payable to the Central government.

(b) State Goods and Service Tax/Union Territory Goods and Service Tax (SGST/UTGST), which is payable to the state government/government of union territory, as the case may be.

Therefore, in the above case, the total GST rate would be CGST+SGST/UTGST.

2. For supply of goods and services from one State to another, i.e. for inter-state supply, GST would be applicable as:

   Integrated Goods and Service Tax (IGST), which is payable to the Central government.

The rate of IGST would be equal to CGST+SGST/UTGST rates applicable on that product.

A pictorial representation of the structure of GST is shown in Figure 1.1:

FIGURE 1.1

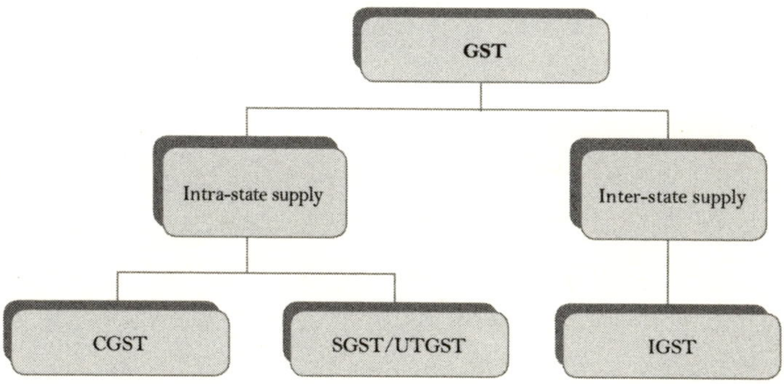

The structure of GST in Figure 1.1 resolves the issue of distribution of tax revenue between states and the centre. Revenue of IGST would be apportioned between the state and centre on the basis recommended by the GST council.

Journey of GST

You said earlier that it took GST 17 long years to see the light of day. What took so long?

Constitutional Amendment

Introducing GST in a country like India was never easy. In a quasi-federal country like ours, where powers are divided between the Centre and states, bringing in a big tax reform like GST meant ensuring the whole nation was on board before its implementation.

The Central government and the state governments derive the power to levy tax from the Constitution of India. The Constitution, prior to the introduction of GST, had three lists for division of powers (including the power to levy tax), viz.:

LIST I: Enumerates subjects where the Central Government has the power to legislate—including the power to levy taxes on manufacture of goods, provision of service, levy of customs duties, etc.

LIST II: Enumerates subjects where the state governments have the power to legislate—including the power to levy taxes on sale of goods.

LIST III: Enumerates subjects where both the Central government and state governments have the power to legislate—such as the power to make laws on education or forestation.

The lists clearly demonstrate that exclusive power used to be given either to the Central government or to the state governments to impose tax on each subject. However, under GST, every transaction in the supply chain (right from the manufacturing stage to distribution to end consumers) is taxed both by the Central government and state governments (i.e. every transaction would include both CGST and SGST). In order to make this happen, the Constitution of India had to be amended so that simultaneous powers could be given to both Central and state governments to tax all transactions. In the absence of such an amendment, GST would have no legal validity.

However, amending the constitution is no mean task. A change in a constitution like ours requires a bill to be passed by both houses of parliament and ratification by more than 50% of the states. A lot of states had initially resisted GST because of the purported loss of power and revenue, but the Bill was eventually passed by a majority in 2016.

Overhauling the entire indirect tax system of the country could also be possible once the interests of all parties—consumers, industry and government—had been taken care of. A lot of thought went into the GST law before it could be finalised so that it catered to everyone's interests. Once all the glitches had been ironed out and after a few initial hurdles, GST was successfully implemented in India in 2017.

Amendment of the constitution wasn't the only hurdle; the biggest challenge was getting all the states to concur on the finalisation of the GST law—especially since various states were ruled by various different political parties. Empowered Committee (EC) of State Finance Ministers, which was constituted in the year 2007 to pave a road map for implementation of GST, played a very proactive role in finalising various complex issues with the concurrence of all the states. EC was formed by the Central government because states played a very important and decisive role for GST as state taxes were also to be subsumed under GST.

Under the erstwhile tax regime, one of the most difficult areas to tax used to be the inter-state movement of goods. The conceptualisation of IGST, as it exists today, was a brilliant idea, which satisfied all stakeholders. The implementation of GST in a country like ours can only be considered a monumental tax reform—especially considering the many factors against it: different states being ruled by different political parties, historical differences in laws and policies governing different states and the unpreparedness of a vast majority of the SME sector to adopt a technology-based GST. It is little wonder, therefore, that various developed countries of the world as well as international organisations such as the IMF and the World Bank have appreciated the introduction of GST in India.

Oh wow! That's a huge feat that we have achieved! But what happened in these 17 long years before the introduction of GST?

When It All Began

The concept of GST was first introduced by the Vajpayee government in the year 2000. As is the case with every big change, GST faced a lot of resistance. Committees were set up and a lot of research went into finding out what kind of GST model should be implemented in a country like ours. Multiple deliberations, discussions and debates were held, and both expert and public opinion were considered before GST was finally implemented. Its journey has indeed been a tumultuous one and its key points can be seen in the Figure 2.1:

FIGURE 2.1

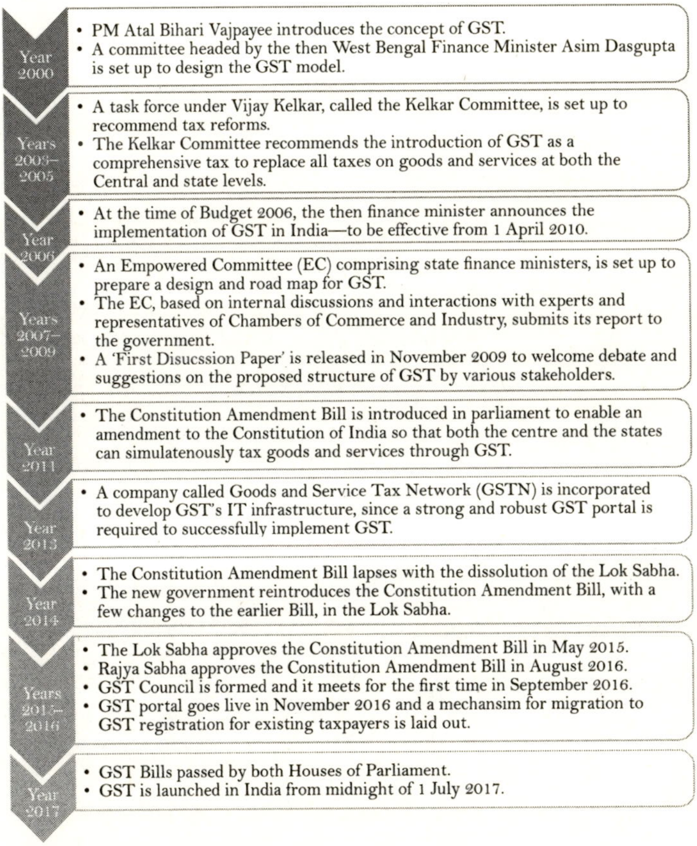

GST in Brief

So, when exactly is GST applicable?

Levying of GST

GST is levied on all transactions which involve the supply of goods and services. Supply includes:

a. All forms of supply of goods or services like: sale, transfer, barter, exchange, license, rental, lease or disposal made by a person for a consideration in the course of or furtherance of business.
b. Import of services for a consideration.
c. Any activity specified by the government as supply, whether or not for consideration.

And what is the rate of GST?

Rate of GST

The rate of GST was determined after a series of calculations so that there was no loss of revenue to either the Central or state governments. An approach called the Revenue Neutral Rate (RNR) was adopted to arrive at the various rates of GST. The RNR was used to calculate the total revenue to Central and state governments from various indirect taxes under the pre-GST regime (such as excise duty, service tax, VAT, etc.). Once this was done, the rate of GST for various products was fixed accordingly so that the total revenue to the government remained the same as it had been in the pre-GST era.

While the GST rates for a few products might seem higher to the consumer than the tax rates of the pre-GST regime, it must be noted that there were a lot of hidden taxes in the earlier regime that were not visible to the end consumer. Today, all of those taxes have been clubbed under a single GST rate. Also, the RNR method has helped to ensure that the ultimate tax burden on the consumer has remained the same, post and pre-GST.

The government has issued notifications, specifying the rates of GST applicable on various goods and services. At present, the notified rates of GST are shown in Figure 3.1:

FIGURE 3.1

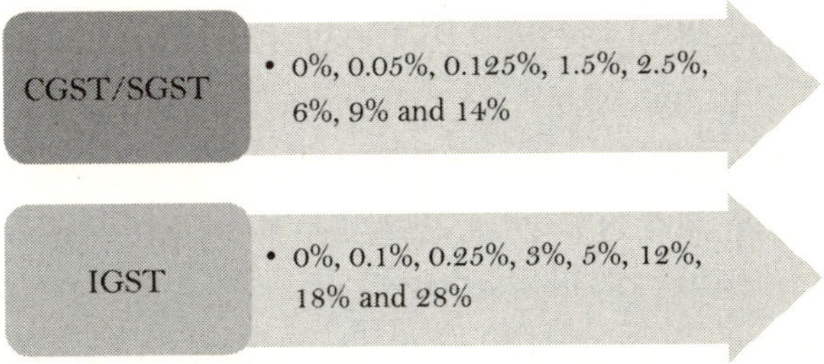

Who deposits GST with the government?

Liability to Pay GST

Forward Charge Mechanism

GST is an indirect tax levy and, therefore, the ultimate burden of GST would be on the end consumer. However, the liability to deposit GST with the government generally rests with the supplier of goods and services.

For example, Mr A sells goods to Mr B. Mr A will collect GST from Mr B, by charging it in his sales invoice and deposit the GST so collected from Mr B to the government within the prescribed time limit. This is known as forward charge mechanism under the GST structure. It is important to note here that, even if Mr B does not make the payment to Mr A, the latter still has to pay taxes to the government. If later, Mr A declares Mr B as bad debt, then Mr A can raise a credit note and claim refund of GST so paid from the government.

Reverse Charge Mechanism

In some cases, the government has placed the responsibility of depositing tax on the recipient of the goods or services. This is known as reverse charge mechanism (RCM), indicating that the recipient is the one who bears the tax and is also the one who deposits it with the government. All rules applicable to the supplier, as far as deposit of tax is concerned, are applicable to the recipient, such as the time within which the tax should be deposited, etc.

A few things that need to be kept in mind under RCM are:

1. Recipient liable to pay tax under RCM is required to obtain registration under GST, even though he/she may have not crossed the threshold limit for obtaining GST registration or may not provide any outward supplies.
2. The recipient has to pay tax through electronic cash ledger only. Input tax credit *(the concept of input tax credit is explained later in the chapter)* cannot be utilised to deposit GST.
3. The recipient is liable to avail input tax credit on GST so deposited.

4. Dealers opting for composition scheme *(the concept of composition scheme is explained in detail in Chapter 10)*, should pay taxes under RCM at the normal rate and not at concessional rate as provided under composition scheme.

Some of the services notified by the Government on which tax is payable by the recipient of service, i.e. under RCM, are:

FIGURE 3.2

Services provided by a Goods Transport Agency to specified persons	Legal services provided by an individual advocate or a firm of advocates	Services provided by an arbitral tribunal to a business entity
Sponsorship services provided to a body corporate or a partnership firm	Specified services provided by Central or state governments or any local authority	Services provided by a director of a company to the said company
Services provided by an insurance agent to a person carrying out insurance business	Services by a recovery agent to a banking or financial company	Services by an author, music composer, photographer, artist, etc., by way of tranfer or by permitting the use of copyright
Services by the members of Overseeing Committee to RBI	Services by individual direct selling agents to bank or banking non-financial company	Services by a person located outside India to any person in India*
	Services of transportation of goods provided by a person located outside India for transporting the goods to India*	

*These are specific situations in which IGST is paid. In other scenarios, depending on whether the supply is inter-state or intra-state, IGST or CGST and SGST would be applicable.

Is there a specific point at which we can say that supply has been made?

Time of Supply

Time of Supply (TOS) is the point at which the liability to charge GST arises. It helps to determine when a supply is made. The GST law provides for different methods to determine time of supply for goods and services, as can be seen in the figure below:

FIGURE 3.3

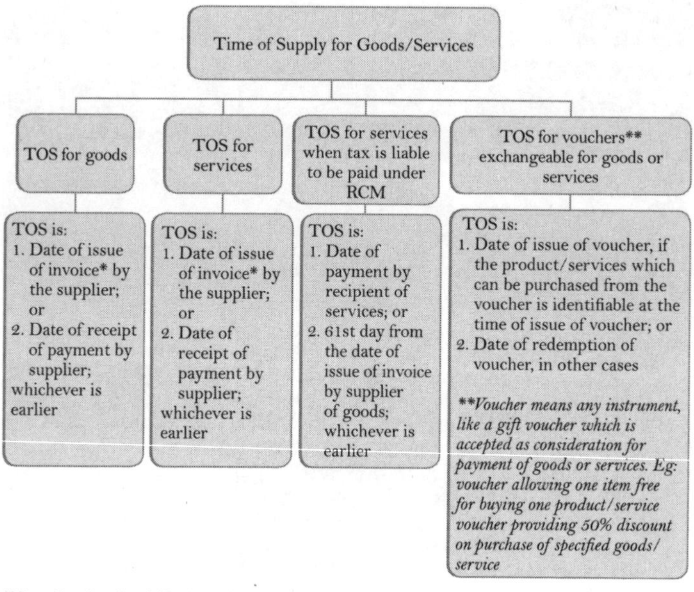

*Note: Invoice should be issued within the time limit prescribed under the GST law.

Okay, so what is the value on which GST should be charged?

Value of Supply

The value of supply on which rate of GST should be applied is the transaction value of goods or services. Normally, the transaction value is the invoice value, i.e. the price actually paid or payable by the recipient of goods or services.

The following points in Table 3.1 should be included while calculating the transaction value:

TABLE 3.1

Inclusions in the Transaction Value (Items to Be Added to Arrive at the Transaction Value)	Exclusions from the Transaction Value
• Any taxes, duties, cesses, fees or charges aplicable under any law, except GST or GST compensation cess • Amount incurred or paid by recipient on behalf of supplier of goods or services • Incidental expenses incurred before supply, such as packing, testing, weightment, etc. • Interest, late fee or penalty for delayed payment of consideration	• Discount is not added to the transaction value if it was known before or at the time of supply (even if given later). However, discounts given after the supply of goods which was not known or contemplated at the time of supply, will not be deducted from the transaction value, and hence, GST would be applicable on such discounts

Inclusions in the Transaction Value (Items to Be Added to Arrive at the Transaction Value)	Exclusions from the Transaction Value
• Subsidies directly linked to the supply are included (i.e. the amount of subsidy should be added to the transaction value). However, subsidies provided by the government are not to be included	

Transaction value (or invoice value) is considered as the basis on which GST can be levied only if the following conditions are fulfilled:

1. Supplier and recipient of goods or services are not related; and
2. Price (i.e. invoice/transaction value) is the only consideration paid for supply of goods or services.

If these two conditions are not fulfilled, then transaction value cannot be considered as the value of supply on which GST would be applicable. In those cases, Value of Supply rules, as notified by the government, would have to be referred to.

Rules for Determination of Value of Supply

#DIY_tip

TABLE 3.2

Sl. No.	Scenarios	Methods to Be Followed for Valuation of Supply (In the Given Order Only)
1.	Taxable value when consideration is not wholly in money	(a) Open market value of supply* or (b) Sum total of monetary consideration plus money value of non-monetary consideration, or (c) Value of supply of like kind and quality of goods or services * It is the full value in money, excluding GST, when buyer and seller are not related and price is the sole consideration. The open market value of a supply should be ascertained at the same time that the supply being valued is made
2.	Taxable value when supply is between related persons (In such cases, there is a chance that the relationship may influence the price of supply, and hence, special valuation rules have been framed)	(a) Open market value of supply* or (b) Value of supply of like kind and quality of goods or services *It may be noted that if the recipient of goods or service is eligible for set-off of full credit of taxes on inputs, then there will be no incentive for undervaluing the transaction and hence the invoice value would be considered as the open market value #GG_tip

»

Sl. No.	Scenarios	Methods to Be Followed for Valuation of Supply (In the Given Order Only)
3.	Value of supply of goods made or received through an agent	Value of supply of goods between the principal and his/her agent shall be: (a) Open market value of goods* or (b) 90% of the price of similar goods sold to unrelated parties by the recipient of the goods
4.	Value of supply of goods or services based on cost	If in the above scenarios, it is not feasible to use the given rules to ascertain the value of supply, then the latter should be 110% of the cost of manufacture/acquisition of goods or provision of service
5.	Residual method for determination of value of supply of goods or services	If none of the above rules are feasible to calculate the value of supply, then the value should be calculated using reasonable means consistent with the general principles of valuation of supply

Value of supply in certain specific cases can be seen in Table 3.3.

#DIY_tip

TABLE 3.3

Sl. No	Scenarios	Methods of Valuation of Supply
1.	Value of supply of services for booking air tickets by a travel agent	Value of taxable supply of services provided by travel agent is: In case of domestic bookings—5% of the basic air fare In case of international bookings—10% of the basic air fare
2.	Value of a token/ voucher/coupon	Transaction value of a coupon/token/ voucher redeemable against goods or service shall be equal to the money value of goods or service redeemed

How do I know when I should charge CGST and SGST or IGST? In other words, how do I know whether a transaction is an inter-state or an intra-state supply?

Place of Supply

The concept of Place of Supply (POS) is relevant to determine whether a transaction is inter-state or intra-state supply. It helps to determine whether goods or services have been provided in the same state or have moved from one state to another. This would help in determining the right tax to be applied on a transaction, viz.: IGST or CGST and SGST. It also helps to determine whether a particular transaction is imports or exports. Tax treatment for imports and exports is different, and hence, POS would help in determining the same.

If a person pays the wrong tax inadvertently, i.e. if a transaction attracts IGST, but he/she pays CGST and SGST on that transaction, then he/she would have to pay the right tax first and claim refund of the tax already paid. However, he/she will not be liable to pay any interest for the correct tax to be paid. This would increase procedural requirements and would even hamper the cashflow. It is, therefore, important to understand the principles of POS and charge correct GST on a transaction to avoid hassles in future.

The GST law provides different rules for determining POS for goods and services. While it is simple to determine POS for goods as they are tangible and their movement from one place to another place can be easily traced, POS for services is a little complicated. Services are intangible and can be provided in various manners, such as from the suppliers' office or at the clients' office or over the internet, etc. Therefore, determining POS for services can be tricky.

Let's discuss POS rules for goods and services below in Table 3.4.

Place of Supply for Goods

TABLE 3.4

Sl. No	Scenarios	Place of Supply
1.	Supply involving movement of goods (Eg: Sale of goods by a trader in Delhi to a buyer in Mumbai)	Location of goods at the place where the goods terminate for delivery to the recipient. (POS is Mumbai, as delivery of goods terminates at Mumbai)

Sl. No	Scenarios	Place of Supply
2.	Supply of goods to a person at the direction of a third person (Eg: Mr X of Delhi places an order with Mr Y of Mumbai to deliver 12 sofa sets to Mr Z of Chennai)	It is deemed that the third person has received the goods and the principal place of business of the third person is the POS. (POS is principal place of business of third person who is Mr X. Therefore, POS is Delhi.)
3.	Supply not involving movement of goods (Eg: Sale of clothes in a mall in Bengaluru)	Location of goods at the time of delivery to the recipient. (POS is Bengaluru)
4.	Where the goods are assembled or installed at site (Eg: Mr A places an order with Mr B of Bengaluru to install a machine in A's factory in Jamnagar, Gujarat)	Place of assembly or installation (POS is Jamnagar, Gujarat)
5.	Goods supplied onboard a conveyance like a vessel, aircraft, train or motor vehicle (Eg: Mr X boards a Delhi–Mumbai train at Delhi. The dinner is loaded into the train at Kota, Rajasthan. Mr X buys dinner at Ratlam station from the train vendor)	Location at which the goods are taken on board. (POS for dinner supplier is Kota)
6.	Residual cases	The government may prescribe rules for such cases

Place of Supply for Services

TABLE 3.5

Sl. No	Scenarios	Place of Supply
1.	General/default rule: When POS is not covered under any of the specific rules mentioned below, then this rule is applicable: (a) Supply made to a person registered under GST (B2B supply) (b) Supply made to unregistered person (B2C supply): (i) Where the address on record exists (ii) In other cases	 Location of registered person (i.e. service recipient) Location of the service recipient Location of supplier of services
2.	Services related to immovable property like hotel accommodation services, construction services, renting, works contract or services of architect, interior decorator, estate agents, engineers, etc.	Location of the immovable property Eg: If an architect from Mumbai provides architectural services for a building in Gujarat, the POS will be Gujarat and it will be treated as inter-state supply If the same architect provides service to a builder registered in Mumbai for his/her new project in London, then POS will be out of India
3.	Restaurant and catering services, personal grooming, fitness, beauty treatment and health services	Location where the services are actually performed

Sl. No	Scenarios	Place of Supply
4.	Services related to training and performance appraisal to: (a) a registered person (B2B supply) (b) an unregistered person (B2C supply)	 Location of service recipient Location where the services are actually performed
5.	Admission to an event (like cultural, sporting, scientific, educational events, etc.) or an amusement park	Place where the event is held or the park is located
6.	Services related to organisation of an event (like cultural, sporting, scientific, educational events) to: (a) a registered person (B2B supply) (b) an unregistered person (B2C supply) (i) if event is held in India (ii) if event is held outside India	 Location of the service recipient Location where event is actually held Location of the service recipient
7.	Transportation of goods, including by courier, provided to: (a) a registered person (B2B supply) (b) an unregistered person (B2C supply)	 Location of the service recipient Location where the goods are handed over for their transportation
8.	Passenger transportation service to: (a) a registered person (B2B supply) (b) an unregistered person (B2C supply)	 Location of the service recipient Place where the passenger first embarks on a continuous journey

»

Sl. No	Scenarios	Place of Supply
9.	Services onboard a conveyance—vessel, aircraft, train or a motor vehicle	Location of the first point of departure of the conveyance for the journey
10.	Telecommunication services: (a) Services by way of leased circuits, telecommunication line, cable or dish antenna (b) Mobile or internet connection provided on post-paid basis (c) Mobile, internet or DTH services provided on pre-paid basis—where recharge is done through electronic mode of payment	 Location where the line/ equipment is installed Billing address of the recipient of service Location of the recipient of services on the record of the supplier of services
11.	Banking and other financial services (including stock broking services)	Location of the service recipient on the record of the supplier of services Where location of recipient of services is not available, POS is location of supplier of services
12.	Insurance services to: (a) a registered person (b) an unregistered person	 Location of the service recipient Location of the service recipient on the record of the supplier of services.
13.	Advertisement services to government	POS is each state or UT for whom the services are availed

Place of Supply for Exports and Imports

TABLE 3.6

Sl. No	Scenarios	Place of Supply
1.	Exports	Location outside India
2.	Imports	Location of importer

Place of Supply in Case of Cross-border Services

In cross-border services, either the location of the supplier or the location of the recipient is outside India. In such cases, the POS of services is as shown in Table 3.7:

TABLE 3.7

Sl. No	Scenarios	Place of Supply
1.	Performance-based services: (a) Services supplied to an individual or services in respect of goods, which require the physical presence of the person/goods (Eg: Ms A, a make-up artist in Chennai, travels to Dubai to provide her services to Ms Z) (b) Services in relation to goods provided from a remote location through electronic means	 Location where the services are actually performed (POS is Dubai, since the services are performed in Dubai) Location of goods at the time of supply of services

»

Sl. No	Scenarios	Place of Supply
2.	Services related to immovable property, like hotel accommodation services or services of architect, interior decorator, estate agents, engineers, etc.	Location of immovable property
3.	Services related to organisation of an event (like cultural, sporting, scientific, educational events, conference, exhibition, etc.) and services ancillary to it	Place where the event is actually held
4.	Banking and other financial services	Location of the service provider
5.	Services by a broker, agent or any intermediary in relation to supply of goods or services or securities between two or more persons	Location of the service provider (i.e. the agent/broker)
6.	Hire of any means of transport including yachts but excluding aircrafts and vessels	Location of the service provider
7.	Transportation of goods (other than by courier)	Place of destination of goods
8.	Passenger transportation services	Place where the passenger embarks on the conveyance for a continuous journey
9.	Services provided onboard a conveyance	Location of the first point of departure of the conveyance for the journey

Sl. No	Scenarios	Place of Supply
10.	Online information and database access or retrieval services (OIDAR): Automated services whose delivery is through electronic commerce and impossible to ensure in the absence of information technology	Location of service recipient
11.	General/residuary provision: When POS is not covered under any of the specific rules mentioned above	Location of service recipient If location of service recipient is not available, then POS would be location of supplier of service

One of the reasons we need GST, you mention, is 'seamless flow of tax credits'. Can you tell me more?

Input Tax Credit

So, input tax credit means the availability of credit of taxes paid on inputs (goods, services or capital goods) procured. Under GST, tax is levied at every stage of the consumer chain. A typical consumer chain for supply of goods may look like Figure 3.4.

FIGURE 3.4

Typically, any goods which reaches the ultimate consumer, goes through the stages in Figure 3.4. GST is levied on supply of goods at each stage as it passes through the consumer chain.

(Generally, in case of supply of services, there is just a service provider who directly provides services to the service recipient.)

The levy of GST is based on 'value added'. That means GST at each stage should be levied only on the value added at that stage—and not on the whole value again, as that would lead to tax on tax.

For example, a manufacturer produces soap and sells it to the distributor for ₹100. The manufacturer would charge GST at the rate of 18% on ₹100 and the final price charged (including GST) to the distributor would be ₹118 (100 + 18% of 100). GST in this transaction is ₹18.

The distributor then re-packs the bulk packing of soap into smaller packs and sells it to a wholesaler for ₹125 (this includes the distributor's profit margin too). He/she would charge GST at the rate of 18% on ₹125 and the final price charged (including GST) to the wholesaler would be ₹147.5 (125 + 18% of 125). GST in this transaction is ₹22.5.

In the case of the distributor, we can see that GST is levied twice on the basic value of soap (which is ₹100)—once in the hands of the manufacturer and then again, in the hands of the distributor. To avoid this taxation of a product more than once, GST is based on the concept of 'value added'.

Continuing with the above example, the distributor would charge GST in his/her invoice to the wholesaler as ₹22.5; however, while depositing tax with the government, the distributor would deposit only ₹4.5 (22.5 - 18). This means that the distributor has received credit of GST (tax) paid on inputs (i.e. soap) procured by him/her against his/her output liability of further selling the soaps to the wholesaler. This way, tax is levied only once on the basic value—and at the stage of the distributor, tax is levied only on value added. This is input tax credit.

Let's take the example further. The wholesaler procures soaps from the distributor and sells it further to the retailer after adding his/her margin, say at ₹153. He/she would charge GST on said price at the rate of 18% and sell it to the retailer at a price inclusive of GST at ₹180.5 (153 + 18% of 153). GST in this transaction, therefore, is ₹27.5. In this case, while depositing GST with the government, the wholesaler would deposit tax of ₹5 (27.5 - 22.5), thus, taking credit of tax paid on procurement of inputs and, thereby, paying tax only on the 'value added' portion of the transaction.

This is how tax is levied only on the 'value added' portion of the entire consumer chain.

Thus, we can conclude that input tax credit is the availability of set-off of taxes paid on procurement of inputs or input services from the output tax liability of a person.

In the earlier regime, different taxes were levied at different stages of the consumer chain. When a manufacturer sold goods, he/she would levy excise duty on the manufactured goods. When the distributor sold goods to the wholesaler, VAT would be levied. Excise duty was levied only at the stage of manufacture and not at distribution stage. Since both excise duty and VAT were levied under different laws and came under different governments (Central and state), no credit of excise duty paid on procurement of goods was available against VAT liability to be paid when goods were further sold. This led to excise duty forming part of the cost of procurement of goods and VAT was levied on a value inclusive of excise duty. This led to a situation of tax on tax, commonly known as the cascading effect of taxes. Under GST, however, since only one tax is levied throughout the value chain, the credits flow seamlessly and, hence, avoid the cascading effect of taxes.

Conditions That Must Be Satisfied for ITC

The conditions that need to satisfied if a person wants to avail ITC are:

1. *Goods or Services to Be Used for Business Purposes*: Only goods or services procured for use in the course or for furtherance of business are eligible for ITC. Tax paid on goods or services availed for non-business purposes cannot be used as ITC.
2. *Possession of Relevant Tax-paying Documents*: A person should have a tax invoice issued by the supplier or a bill of entry (in case of imports) or any other specified tax-paying documents to avail ITC. Amongst other things, these documents should have the GSTIN of the supplier, total value of goods or services, amount of tax charged, etc., for it to be a valid document for claiming ITC.

3. *Receipt of Goods or Services*: A purchaser should have actually received goods or services before claiming ITC. Delivery to any other person, at the instruction of the purchaser of goods/services is also considered as receipt of goods.
4. *Tax Charged is Actually Paid to the Government by the Supplier*: A purchaser can claim ITC only when the tax is actually deposited with the government by the supplier of goods or services.However, a purchaser can claim provisional ITC initially to settle his/her outward tax liability.
5. *The Purchaser Should Have Filed Their Return*: To claim ITC, details of purchases of goods or services should be provided in the GST return.
6. *Payment of Invoice by Purchaser Is Not Made Within 180 Days from Date of Invoice*: If the purchaser has not paid the supplier of goods or services within 180 days from the date of invoice, then any ITC claimed by the purchaser basis the tax invoice should be reversed and added to the purchaser's output tax liability, along with interest at the specified rate. In this case, the purchaser is eligible to take re-credit of ITC when the purchaser has made the payment of invoice to the supplier.

Time Limit to Claim ITC

A purchaser is required to avail ITC in the return before:

1. The due date of furnishing of GST return for the month of September of the following financial year, or
2. Furnishing the annual return of the current financial year, whichever is earlier.

For example, if a purchaser has to avail ITC of ₹1,00,000 for the financial year 2018–19, the time limit would be:

1. 20 October 2019 (last date for filing of return for the month of September of the following financial year), or
2. 31 December 2019 (last date for filing annual return of FY 2018–19), whichever is earlier.

Note: In the above example, the last day for filing the return is taken. This means, that a purchaser cannot claim ITC beyond that date. However, in order to calculate the actual time limit, one should consider the actual dates of filing of returns and not the last date of filing. A taxpayer may file annual returns before filing the return for September of the next financial year. In such cases, the date for claiming ITC should be accordingly calculated.

Blocked Credit

Under GST, ITC is available on almost all the goods or services procured by the recipient. However, there are a few exceptions where ITC is not available. These are illustrated in Figure 3.5.

FIGURE 3.5

Purchase of motor vehicles or other conveyances, except if they are purchased for the following:

1. Further sale of such motor vehicle. Eg: purchase by a dealer of cars
2. Transportation of passengers. Eg: purchase of car by Uber
3. Imparting training on such vehicle. Eg: puchase of car by a driving school

Goods or services used for personal consumption, like: beauty parlour services, health services, etc.

If goods or services are procured for construction of immovable property for own use, then no ITC is available on such goods or services. But ITC is allowed to a developer using goods or services for construction of flats for further sale

Any goods which are stolen or destroyed are not eligible for ITC

Any goods which are distributed as gifts or free samples are not eligible for ITC

Apportionment of ITC

Pro-rata apportionment of credit has to be done in certain cases:

1. *Where Goods or Services Procured Are Partly Used for Business and Partly for Non-business Purposes*: As discussed earlier, ITC is not available if the inputs are used for non-business purposes. In a case where inputs are used partly for business and partly for other purposes, credit will have to be apportioned on pro-rata basis—as is attributable to the purposes of business. In other words, ITC will be available only for that portion of inputs which are used for business purposes.
2. *Where Goods or Services Procured Are Partly Used for Effecting Taxable Supply and Partly for Exempt Supply:* Where the supply is exempt from GST, no outward liability to pay GST arises for the taxpayer. In these cases, since there is no outward liability, the taxpayer is also not allowed to claim ITC on inputs procured.

   In a case where inputs are procured to effect both taxable (including exports) and exempt supplies, ITC on inputs so procured would be apportioned on a pro-rata basis as is attributable to taxable supplies. In other words, ITC will be available only for that portion of inputs which has gone into making taxable supplies.

Utilisation of ITC

ITC availed can be utilised to discharge the outward tax liability of a person. However, the credit has to be utilised only in the manner shown in Table 3.8:

#DIY_tip

TABLE 3.8

Input Tax Credit of	To Be Utilised First for Discharging the Liability of	Remaining Credit May Be Utilised for Discharging the Liability of
CGST	IGST	CGST
SGST/ UTGST	IGST	SGST/UTGST
IGST	IGST	CGST, then SGST/UTGST

GST Network/GST Service Provider

GG, I keep reading about GSTN in newspapers. What is it?

Goods and Services Tax Network

In 2010, when discussions for structure and other aspects of GST were being discussed, it was realised that a strong and robust IT infrastructure would be required for its successful implementation. It was then decided that a company should be created to take special care of GST's IT infrastructure. A company called Goods and Services Tax Network (GSTN) was, therefore, incorporated. GSTN is a not-for-profit, non-government company, promoted jointly by the Central and state governments.

At present, the Central and state governments hold 49% stake in the company, while the remaining

51% is held by five private financial institutions—HDFC, HDFC Bank, ICICI Bank, NSE Strategic Investment Company and LIC Housing Finance Ltd. GSTN was created as a non-government organisation so as to allow the company adequate flexibility and freedom to hire the best people and pay the required amount of emoluments and also to ensure timely implementation of IT infrastructure.

Recently, however, the government has decided to convert GSTN into a government holding. It was decided that the Central government would hold 50% stake in GSTN, with the remaining 50% to be held by state governments on a pro-rata basis in their GST revenue. This, the government claimed, would make it easier to save the GSTN portal from cyber attacks while keeping taxpayers' business data safe and prevent it from leaking and misuse.

But why exactly do we need GSTN?

Need for GSTN

GSTN's main purpose is to provide a uniform interface for the taxpayer and a common and shared IT infrastructure between the Central and state governments. In the earlier regime, both Central and state governments worked under different laws, regulations, procedures and formats and, hence, they had independent websites as separate IT systems. Under GST, however, everything has to be brought under one umbrella so that all the tax administrations are at the same level of IT maturity—and that is a humongous and complex task.

GSTN will not only facilitate business processes like obtaining registration, payment of taxes and filing of return, but also help government authorities to obtain data from GSTN and interact with taxpayers when it comes to approval of registration, assessment of return, conducting enquiries, audit and investigation among other things. It will essentially serve as an interface between the government and the taxpayers. The purpose of GSTN is to create a GST ecosystem which will link all stakeholders like government, taxpayers, tax professionals, banks, accounting authorities and others.

To answer the above requirements, GSTN developed the Common GST Electronic Portal—www.gst.gov.in—a common portal for all GST-related services. It can be accessed over the internet by taxpayers and tax professionals, and over the intranet by tax officials.

What can we use the GST common portal for?

Services Rendered by GSTN

GSTN is a one-stop-destination for taxpayers and tax authorities. The former need to only visit the portal to find answers to anything related to GST—be it GST rules, regulations, compliances or anything else. The portal is user-friendly and one can easily navigate their way through it. It also provides user manuals, videos and FAQs regarding various procedures that a taxpayer may undertake, such as filing returns, making GST payments, applying for a refund, filing applications for assessment/appeal/advance ruling, etc.

GSTN also helps tax authorities with a lot of GST work related to the taxpayer—reviewing applications and returns and performing other tax administration-related work.

Some of the services that GSTN provides or the functions that can be performed through common GST electronic portal are shown in Figure 4.1:

FIGURE 4.1

Facilitating application for registration under GST	Payment management for paying taxes (including penalties, fines, interest, etc.) electronically	Uploading of invoice data and filing of various returns or annual statements
Processing of various returns or applications filed on the portal	Running the matching engine for matching, reversal and reclaim of input tax credit	Computation and settlement of IGST between centre and states
Filing and processing of refund under GST	Processing and reconciliation of GST on import and integration with the systems of Customs	Taxpayer management such as, account management, notification, information and status tracking
Tax authorities can perform assessment/ audit/appeal/ investigation, etc. through the portal	Providing analysis of tax payers' profiles to the tax authorities	Providing various MIS reports to the tax authorities based on return information of the taxpayer
	Provide training to stakeholders	

GSTN seems to be a robust platform where all things related to GST are available on a single platform. Can the government also catch taxpayer frauds through GSTN?

What's New under GSTN?

Deeply laid frauds cannot be determined prima facie through the data available on the GSTN database. In fact, tax officers have to dig deep to determine frauds. However, if some news reports are to be believed, the government is at least taking a step towards early detection of frauds. The government has invited bids to hire private entities to develop a Fraud Analytics System. These entities would need to build a 360-degree profiling of taxpayers for early detection of GST evasion and frauds. The profiles would be created using existing taxpayer data already available on GSTN (like registration details, returns filing, e-way bill, history of the owner of the company, change of promoters of a company, etc.) This system would also analyse information of the taxpayer from other external sources such as Financial Intelligence Unit (FIU), Central Board of Direct Taxes (CBDT), banks and state tax departments. The fact that GST registration is also PAN-based will make it easier to gather taxpayer information from all angles.

The private entity engaged with the project would also be required to suggest ways to prevent revenue leakage and suggest changes in GST law to plug loopholes in order to avoid further frauds. They would also need to forecast revenue growth for the government and provide other relevant analyses for policy making on the basis of data analytics done under the project.

To put all worries to rest, the government will take adequate steps to ensure full confidentiality of taxpayers' data while developing and running such a system.

Who has developed the GSTN network?

GSTN has engaged Infosys as the single Managed Service Provider (MSP) for the design, development and deployment of the GST portal. Infosys has developed the application software and the entire IT infrastructure. It is also responsible for operating and maintaining the system for a period of five years from the Go-Live date, i.e. 1 July2017.

That was quite some insightful gyan on GSTN! Could you also explain about GSPs?

Sure, why not?

GST Suvidha Provider

A taxpayer can visit the GST portal on the internet and undertake compliances on their own. However, in some cases, they may need help in interacting with formats provided on GSTN. A GST Suvidha Provider or GSP is an enabler that helps taxpayers to comply with the provisions of the GST law through its web platform. GSPs develop applications to be used by taxpayers for interacting with GSTN.

For example, a taxpayer may maintain his/her sales and purchase data on SAP ERP. To upload the sales/ purchase data on GST portal, the data should be in a GST-compliant format. The taxpayer, in this case, may need help of an application which will convert their data into GST-compliant data. This is where GSPs come to the rescue.

GSPs are private companies enlisted by GSTN who develop different types of applications based on taxpayer's needs. GSPs develop applications or dashboards which provide taxpayers with different kinds of interfaces on desktop/mobile and help them to interact easily with GSTN.

How helpful are these GSPs?

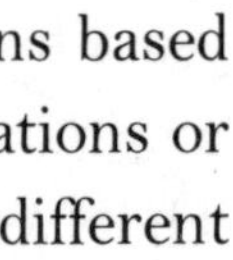

Taxpayer Benefits under GSP

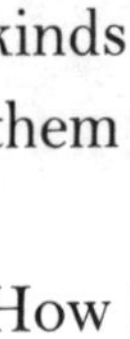

A few benefits that taxpayers may enjoy from using GSPs are listed below:

1. Conversion of current invoice format (which may be in csv, pdf, excel, etc.) to GST-compliant format.
2. Reconciliation of auto populated purchase data on GST portal, with their purchase register. They may both be in different formats and, hence, application for reconciliation may be required.
3. A company registered in multiple states may require a unified view of all branches on one screen.
4. Dashboard for taxpayers to enable quick monitoring of GST compliance activities.
5. Dashboards to view matched/mismatched ITC claims.
6. Large companies may require an automated way to interact with the GST system to upload their invoices directly from their software to the GST portal, as individual uploads of lakhs of invoices may not be possible.
7. GST professionals or GST practitioners may also need some specific applications to manage and undertake GST compliance activities for their clients from one dashboard.

A few months after GST was introduced, it was noted that a lot of listed GSPs were becoming inactive. The ever-changing GST law and the shaky GSTN portal discouraged a lot of GSPs, making them unsure of developing their applications. Another reason that firms were reluctant to be GSPs was that, over time, a few compliance processes were made simpler and taxpayers found that they could manage the compliance and interaction with GSTN themselves without an external application. A lot of taxpayers did their compliances on their own—which was free of cost—rather than relying on their GSP's softwares and paying them money.

Compliances

What are the compliances that we need to undertake under GST?

Some of the basic compliances that need to be undertaken under GST are as follows:

1. Registration
2. Invoicing
3. E-way Bills
4. GST Returns

Let us discuss each point one by one:

I. Registration

The first step of compliance that we need to undertake under GST law is registration. Registration is required to identify the taxpayer and to ensure tax compliance in the economy. Without registration, a person can neither collect GST from his customers nor can he avail the benefit of input tax credit. We shall discuss some of the important aspects of registration in detail below:

1. *No Centralised Registration:* Under the GST regime, if a business entity has branches in multiple states, then separate registrations need to be taken for each state. Unlike in the erstwhile service tax regime, there is no provision for centralised registration under GST.
2. *One Registration Per State:* If a business entity has multiple branches within a state, then it need not take multiple registrations for each branch; a single registration per state is adequate. One place may be declared the principal place of business with others declared as additional places of business.
3. *Registration for Multiple Businesses in a State:* A business entity has an option to obtain separate registration for different business verticals in a state. For example, A Ltd has a factory for the manufacture of cars, another for the manufacture of steel and a trading business of import and sale of steel in a state. A Ltd may either take one combined registration for all three businesses or three separate ones for the three verticals.

Persons Liable to Take Registration under GST

If the aggregate turnover for a supplier exceeds the threshold limit in a financial year, then he becomes liable to take registration. The threshold limit is shown in Table 5.1.

TABLE 5.1

Category	Threshold Limit (in INR)	Threshold Limit in Special Category States* (in INR)
Supplier of Goods	40 lakh	20 lakh
Supplier of Services	20 lakh	10 lakh

**Special Category States include Arunachal Pradesh, Assam, Manipur, Meghalaya, Mizoram, Nagaland, Sikkim, Tripura, Uttarakhand, Himachal Pradesh and Jammu and Kashmir*

Aggregate turnover is computed on an all-India basis for a person with the same Permanent Account Number (PAN). The Table 5.2 lists the items to be included and excluded to calculate the aggregate turnover of a taxpayer:

#DIY_tip

TABLE 5.2

Inclusions	Exclusions
All supplies which are taxable under GST law	Value of all purchases on which tax was paid on reverse charge basis
All supplies of goods and services which are exempt under GST law	All taxes including cess paid under GST law (like CGST, SGST, IGST, UGST)
Exports of goods and/or services	Any interest income on loans or advances made by a person
All inter-state supplies	

Persons Exempt from Taking Registration

The following persons are not required to take registration under GST:

1. Person exclusively supplying goods or services which are exempt from GST, i.e., a person dealing in goods or services which are either outside the ambit of GST or attract nil rate of GST.
2. An agriculturist, i.e., a person engaged in supplying produce out of cultivation of land.
3. Person making supply of goods or services, tax on which is liable to be paid by recipient on reverse charge basis.

Compulsory Registration

The following category of persons is mandatorily required to take registration under GST, that is, the threshold limit does not apply to the following categories of persons:

1. Persons making inter-state supply of goods. However, threshold limit applies to service providers making inter-state supply.
2. A casual taxable person, i.e., a person who occasionally undertakes supplies in a state where he has no fixed place of business.

3. A person who is required to pay tax under reverse-charge mechanism.
4. Non-resident persons making taxable supply.
5. A person who is required to deduct TDS (i.e., Tax Deducted at Source).
6. A person who is supplying goods through Electronic Commerce Operator like a person selling his goods through Flipkart or Amazon.
7. An Electronic Commerce Operator.

How can we take registration under GST?

GST registration is taken online through the GSTN portal. And the registration certificate is also received online by the applicant.

Let us briefly discuss the steps to take registration under GST.

#DIY_tip

Step 1: Go to www.gst.gov.in
Step 2: Go to 'Services' >
'Registration> 'New Registration'

FIGURE 5.1

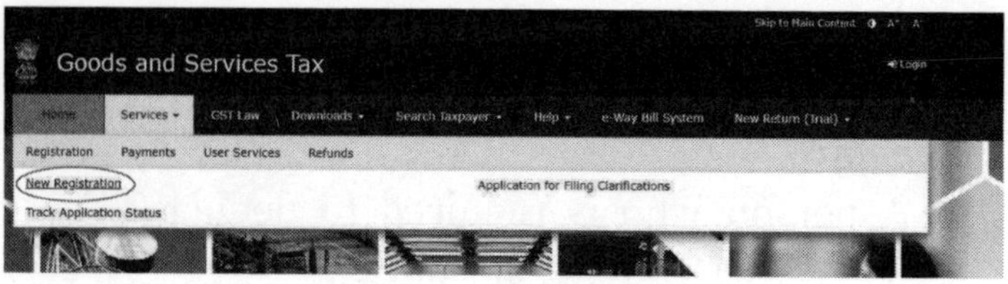

Step 3: The return form is divided into two parts, viz. Part A and Part B.

PART A:

Select 'New Registration'.

Fill in all the relevant details in the given form.

Select 'Proceed'

FIGURE 5.2

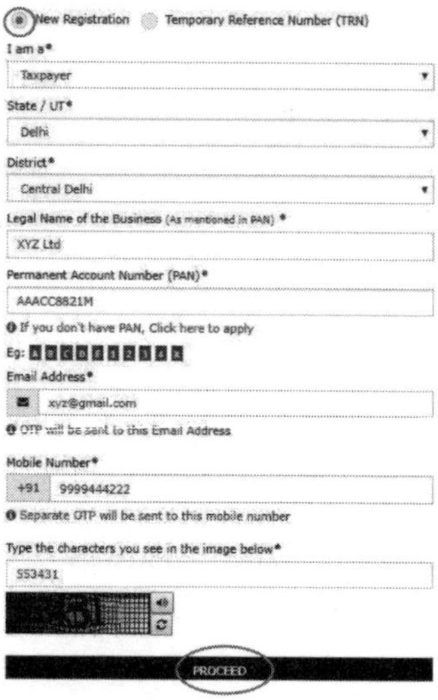

Step 4: An OTP would be sent on mobile and email. Enter both the OTPs and select 'Proceed'

FIGURE 5.3

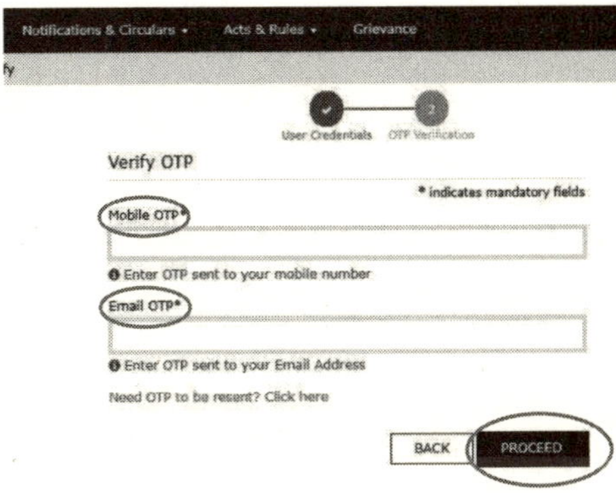

Step 5: An acknowledgment for filing Part A of the form will be displayed.

A TRN would be generated. Please note this TRN, as it is necessary for filing Part B of the registration form

Click 'Proceed' to fill Part B of the form

FIGURE 5.4

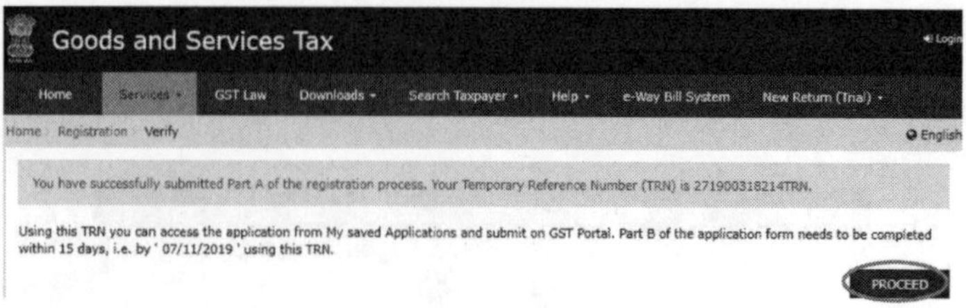

PART B

(Please note that Part B of the form should be submitted within 15 days of filing Part A form, otherwise Part A form would become invalid, and the form would have to be filled afresh)

Step 6: An OTP would be sent on registered email id or mobile number. Enter the OTP and click 'Proceed'.

Enter TRN and click 'Proceed'

FIGURE 5.5

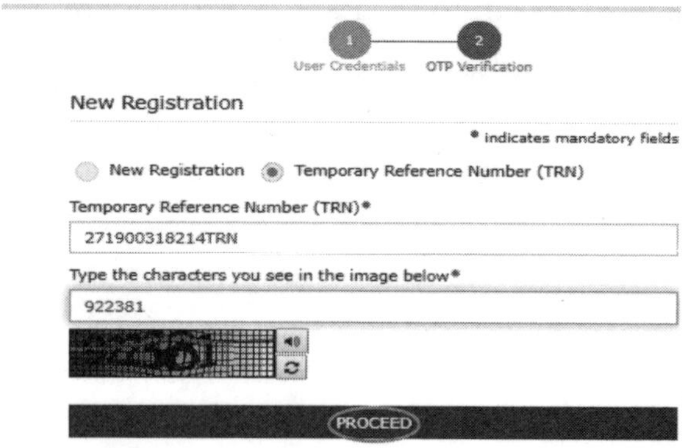

Step 7: Click on the Action button to start filling the form.

FIGURE 5.6

Step 8: Part B of the form has 9 tabs as shown in the Figure 5.7 below. Each tab is to be filled in individually.

While filling the form, option from the dropdown list should be chosen wherever the same is provided for.

Once each tab is filled click on 'Save & Continue' to move on to the next tab. This step is necessary otherwise the data filled in the tab would not be saved when the next tab is opened.

FIGURE 5.7

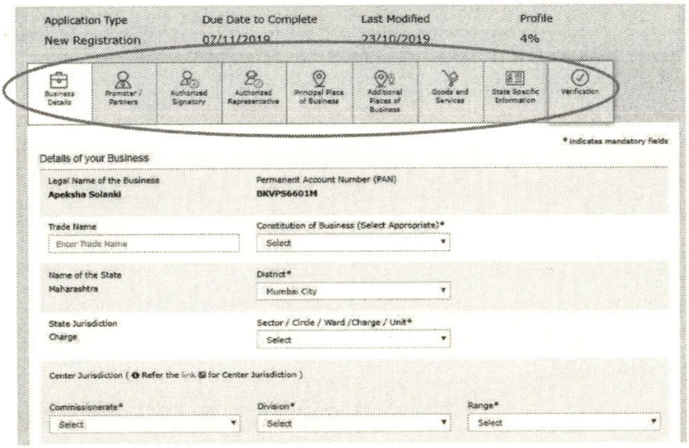

>>

FIGURE 5.7

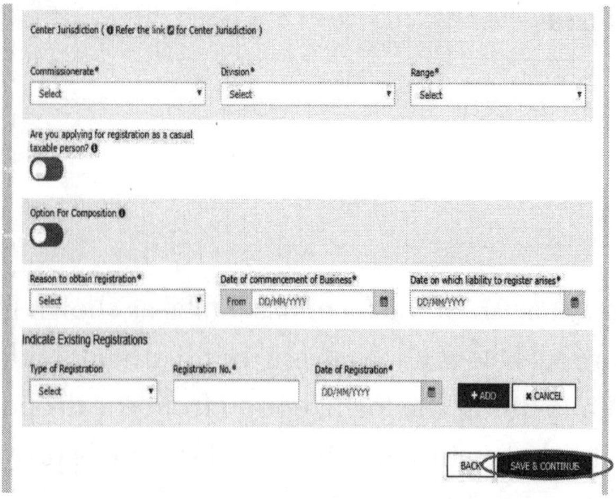

Step 9: As each tab is filled, a small tick appears on the top right corner, as shown in the Figure 5.8 below.

Once all the tabs are filled, go to the 'Verification' tab and submit the form with either of the options available.

FIGURE 5.8

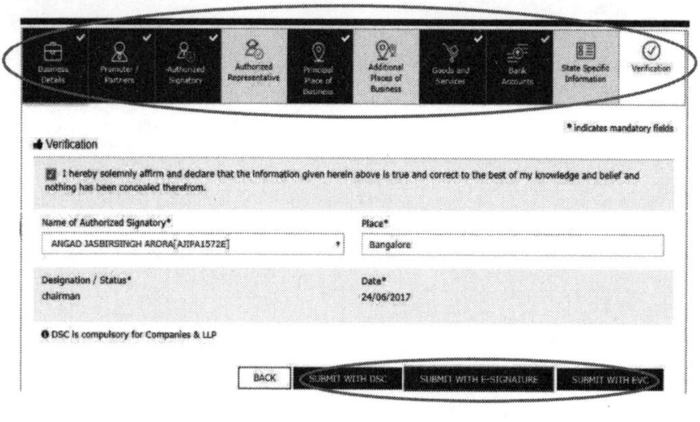

Step 10: Once the form is submitted an acknowledgment and Application Reference Number (ARN) would be sent within 15 minutes on registered mobile number and email id. This ARN can be used to track the status of the application filed.

To track the status of the form submitted, on the homepage go to 'Services'> 'Registration'> 'Track application Status'

FIGURE 5.9

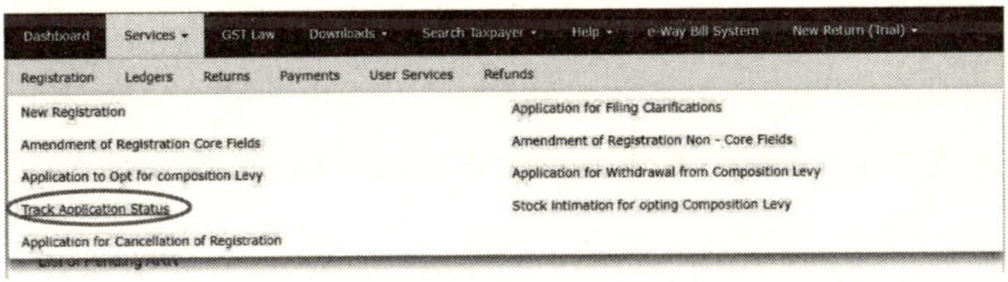

If no communication has been received by the applicant within three working days of submission of the Part B of the registration form, then the registration application is deemed to have been granted to him/her.

Let us now discuss the 2nd important compliance that a taxpayer should undertake.

II. Invoicing

An invoice is a commercial instrument issued by a seller to a buyer and acts as a document, evidencing the payment for goods or services. Under GST, the issuance of an invoice is very significant for the availability of input tax credit. Input tax credit can be availed only if there is an invoice evidencing payment of tax by the buyer and the matching of the invoice of purchase supplies of the buyer with the sales invoice of the seller.

A tax invoice to be issued under GST law should typically have the following contents:

1. Name, address and GSTIN of the supplier.
2. A consecutive serial number, in one or multiple series, unique for a financial year.
3. Date of issue of invoice.
4. Name, address and GSTIN of the recipient.
5. HSN code of goods or Accounting Code of Services.
6. Description of goods or services.
7. Quantity of goods supplied.
8. Total value of supply of goods or services.
9. Taxable value of supply of goods or services, taking into account the discount or abatement, if any.

10. Rate of tax.
11. Amount of tax charged in respect of taxable goods or services.
12. Address of delivery if the same is different from the recipient of supply.
13. Whether the tax is payable on reverse charge basis.
14. Signature or digital signature of the supplier or his authorised representative.
15. Such other details as prescribed under GST law.

Time Limit for Issuance of Tax Invoice

A supplier of goods or services should issue the invoice within the prescribed timelines as given in Figure 5.10.

FIGURE 5.10

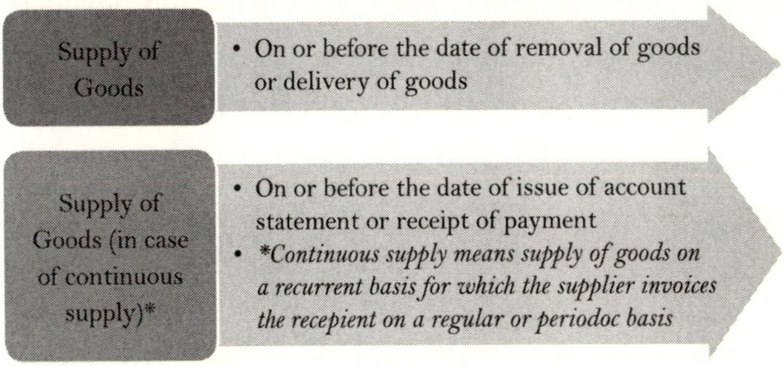

Supply of Services	• In general cases: Within 30 days from the date of supply of service • In case of insurers and banks, financial institution, telecom operator and other specified class of taxpayers: Within 45 days from the date of supply of service
Supply of Services (in case of continuous supply)*	• Where the due date of payment is mentioned in the contract: On or before the due date of payment • Where the due date of payment is not mentioned in the contract: Before or at the time when supplier recieves the payment • **Continuous supply means supply of services on a recurrent basis for a period exceeding 3 months with periodic payment obligations*

Types of Instruments Under GST

Different transactions require the issuance of different types of instruments. GST law prescribes various instruments that a taxpayer may issue to evidence and document supply of goods or services or receipt of payment. Some of these instruments are discussed below:

1. *Receipt Voucher:* When a supplier receives advance payment for supply of goods or services, he may issue a receipt voucher, containing details as may be prescribed, evidencing receipt of such payment.

2. *Refund Voucher:* If a supplier receives advance payment, but subsequently no supply is made, then the supplier may issue to the person who had made the payment a refund voucher against the payment so made.
3. *Bill of Supply:* If a person supplies exempted or non-taxable goods or services or opts to pay tax under composition scheme, he shall issue a bill of supply instead of a tax invoice. The contents of a bill of supply are very similar to a regular tax invoice. One of the major differences is that bill of supply does not contain details pertaining to rate of tax and amount of tax.
4. *Delivery Challan:* GST law prescribes cases where goods can be transported for delivery to the recipient without the issuance of tax invoice. In such cases, the consignor has to issue a delivery challan and tax invoice can be issued by the supplier after delivery of goods. In the following cases it is permissible for the consignor to issue a delivery challan in lieu of invoice at the time of removal of goods:
   (a) Supply of liquid gas where the quantity at the time of removal from the place of business of the supplier is not known.
   (b) Transportation of goods for job work.

(c) Transportation of goods for reasons other than by way of supply, like removal of goods for sale on approval basis.
(d) Such other supplies as may be notified by the GST Board.

5. *Credit and Debit Notes:* If a tax invoice has been issued for a supply and it is subsequently found that the value of goods or services or tax charged in that invoice is more than what is actually payable/chargeable, or if the recipient has returned the goods, then the supplier can issue a credit note to the recipient.

For example, let's say, a supplier raises a bill of ₹10,100 to the buyer. He subsequently realises that the bill amount should have been ₹10,000; he may then issue a credit note to the buyer for ₹100 for the extra amount he inadvertently charged in his/her original tax invoice.

If a tax invoice has been issued for a supply and it is subsequently found that the value of goods or services or tax charged in that invoice is less than what is actually payable/chargeable, then the supplier can issue a debit note to the recipient.

For example, let's say, a supplier raises a bill of ₹9,900 to the buyer. He subsequently

> realises that the actual bill amount should have been ₹10,000; he may then issue a debit note to the buyer for ₹100 for the lesser amount that he inadvertently charged in his original tax invoice.

Any person who issues a credit or debit note in relation to supply of goods or services shall declare the details of such credit or debit note in their GST return and their tax liability shall be adjusted in such manner as may be prescribed.

Thank you, GG, for the detailed gyan on invoicing. Shall we now move on to the next point?

Sure!

III. Electronic Way Bill

One of the biggest achievements of GST has been hassle-free and faster movement of goods across the country. Under the erstwhile regime, a lot of time and cost was involved in movement of goods across or within the states because of the border check posts. Living up to its tagline 'One nation, One tax,

One market', GST has introduced the concept of Electronic Way Bill (E-way bill) which has helped in quick and easy movement of goods across India; all checkposts have now been abolished and goods can be transported across borders (inter-state and intra-state) only on an E-way bill.

An E-way bill is an electronic document generated on the GST portal evidencing movement of goods. It is a mechanism to ensure that goods being transported comply with the GST law and is an effective tool to track movement of goods and check tax evasion. It is a compliance mechanism, whereby, a taxpayer, prior to movement of goods, informs the tax department of the details of goods which are being transported. This way, the transporter does not have to stop at every border checkpost and the verification of goods being transported can be done easily as details of the goods are uploaded on a common portal through internet by way of generation of E-way bill.

E-way bill is generated on the common portal www.ewaybillgst.gov.in in Form GST EWB 01. It can also be generated through other modes like:

1. SMS facility.
2. Using an android app.

3. Using a bulk upload tool.
4. Using site to site integration.

Details of how to use each of these methods can be found on the E-way bill common portal under the 'Help' section under 'FAQs'.

A taxpayer who wishes to generate E-way bill should be a registered person under GST and should also register at the e-way bill portal. Once an E-way bill is generated, the supplier, recipient and the transporter can view, verify and track the E-way bill on the common portal.

An E-way bill has two components: Part A, comprising details of GSTIN of recipient, place of delivery, invoice or challan number and date, value of goods, HSN code and reasons for transportation; and Part B, comprising transporter details like vehicle number and transport document number (Goods Receipt Number or Railway Receipt Number or Airway Bill Number or Bill of Lading Number).

An E-way bill should be generated by a registered person who causes movement of goods (i.e., either the supplier or the recipient of the goods) for consignment value of more than ₹50,000 (inclusive of GST, while the total consignment value should be exclusive of value of GST exempted goods). Every transporter is required to carry a copy of invoice or bill of supply along with E-way bill while transporting the goods. It is important to note here that E-way bill is required even if goods are being transported by rail/air/vessel. GST law also provides exception in case of certain goods, where E-way bill is not required to be generated.

Wow! E-way bill definitely seems very revolutionary!

Shall we now discuss the last point under compliances?

Yes of course, why not?

IV. GST Returns

Filing of returns is the most important compliance procedure which helps the tax department to collect financial data and other relevant information of a registered person. It helps the tax department to build a database which will help track the taxpayers and ensure proper compliance with law is taking place.

Return filing works as a kind of supporting document for tax authorities to verify that the tax paid by the registered person has been calculated correctly. It also helps in determining and tracking the authenticity of the suppliers and vendors a registered person filing the return deals with.

Under GST, various return formats are prescribed for various categories of taxpayers. A few of these are described briefly below in Table 5.3.

TABLE 5.3

Return Form	Description	Frequency	Standard Due Date*
GSTR – 1	Statement of sales of goods and services	Monthly	10th of the next month
GSTR – 2A	Auto-populated details of purchases made available to a buyer on the basis of form GSTR-1 furnished by the supplier	Monthly	11th of the next month
GSTR – 2 (Not operationalised so far)	Statement of purchases of goods and services *(any addition or modification in form GSTR-2A should be filed in GSTR-2)*	Monthly	15th of the next month
GSTR – 3 (Not operationalised so far)	Monthly return filed on the basis of finalisation of details of sales and purchases along with payment of tax	Monthly	20th of the next month

Return Form	Description	Frequency	Standard Due Date*
GSTR – 3B	Simplified monthly return in which summary of sales, purchases, total tax payable, details of input tax credit utilised and tax paid in cash is declared by the taxpayer	Monthly	20th of the next month
GSTR – 4	Return form for person opting to pay tax under composition scheme	Annual	30th April of the succeeding year
GSTR – 5	Return for a non-resident taxpayer	Monthly	20th of the next month
GSTR –8	Statement furnished by e-commerce operator for depicting supplies effected through it on which tax was collected at source	Monthly	10th of the next month
GSTR – 9	Annual return comprising summary of various details filed in periodic returns filed during the year and additional declarations like transactions of previous year declared in next year, HSN wise summary, along with differential tax payment made, if any	Annually	31st December of next financial year

**The government may extend the time limit to file a particular return for a particular period by issuing a notification.*

It may be noted that as per the GST law, a normal taxpayer is required to file three returns every month, viz.: GSTR-1, 2 & 3. However, the government has kept filing of GSTR-2 & 3 on hold as of now for letting the tax payers ease into the GST compliance process. Instead, a simplified monthly return GSTR-3B has been introduced temporarily for filing summarised details of sales and input tax credit. So, at present, taxpayer has to file only two returns every month, viz.: GSTR-1 & GSTR-3B.

To further ease the compliance process for small taxpayers, government has allowed taxpayers with annual aggregate turnover of up to ₹1.5 crore to file GSTR -1 on quarterly basis, instead of monthly basis. However, filing of GSTR-3B and tax payment has to be made on monthly basis even by small taxpayers. Also, small taxpayers can opt for composition scheme where only annual return is required to be filed. It is pertinent to note that more than 90% taxpayers in the country are covered in the above mentioned two categories.

Secondly, since GST returns require filing of invoice level information, it may seem a little overwhelming for small taxpayers. However, it is worthwhile to mention that only invoices of B2B sales (business to business where buyer intends to avail credit of tax paid by supplier) are required to be entered in GSTR 1. Details of sales made on B2C basis (business to consumer where buyer consumes the goods and do not intend to avail credit of tax paid by supplier) are not required to be entered on invoice level basis.

Let us briefly discuss the process of return filing under GST.

#DIY_tip

Steps to File GSTR-1

Under GST, all returns are filed electronically through any of the following methods:

1. *Online Mode:* GST return can be filed directly on the GST portal.
2. *Offline Mode:* Excel utilities are available on the GST portal. These return utilities can be downloaded and filled offline and once the return is fully prepared, it can be uploaded on the GST website.

Following steps can be followed to file the return through offline mode:

Download offline utility from homepage ('www.gst.gov.in' > 'Downloads' > 'Offline Tools' > 'Returns Offline Tool' > 'Download')

Fill your data in the excel sheet as per given instructions > Login to GST portal > Upload file after clicking 'Prepare Offline'.

3. *GSPs:* Returns can also be filed with the help of a GSP *(as discussed in Chapter 4)*

Let us discuss the detailed steps of filing returns through online mode:

Steps to File GSTR-1:

Step 1: Login to www.gst.gov.in.

Step 2: Go to 'Services' > 'Returns > 'Returns Dashboard'.

Step 3: Select the financial year and return filing period from the dropdown list for which the return is to be filed.

Click 'Search'.

Select the appropriate answer 'Yes' or 'No' to opt for the option of quarterly filing of return. This option is available only if the annual aggregate turnover is less than 1.5 crore.

Click 'Submit'.

FIGURE 5.11

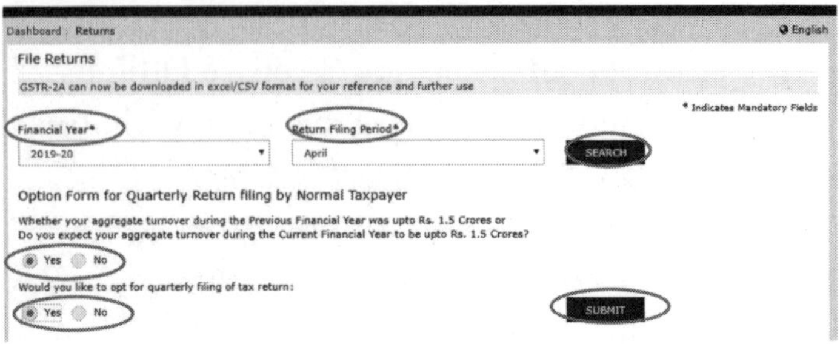

Step 5: Under GSTR-1 tab, click 'Prepare Online'.

FIGURE 5.12

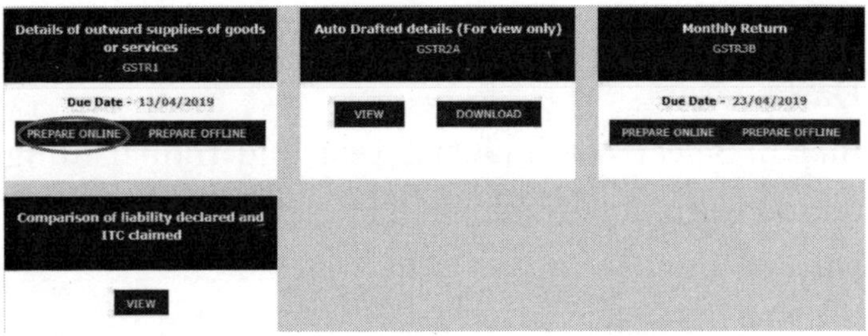

Step 6: The main page of GSTR-1 is displayed.

Enter 'Aggregate Turnover' details.

FIGURE: 5.13

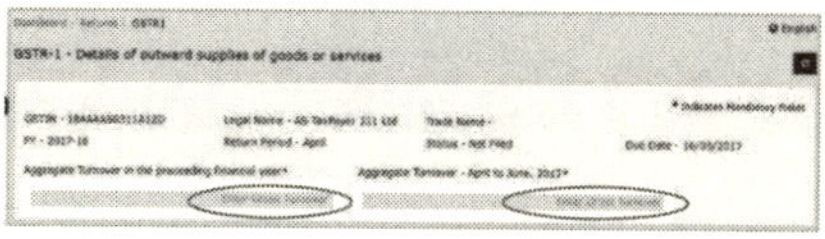

Step 7: Each of the following tabs should be filled in individually with the relevant details. If a particular tab is not applicable to the taxpayer, then that tab may be kept blank.

FIGURE 5.14

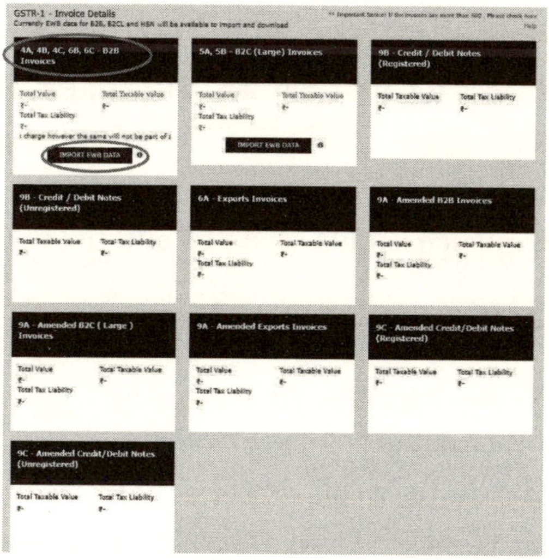

FIGURE 5.15

Step 8: Select the first tab '4A, 4B, 4C, 6B, 6C-B2B invoices'.

Click 'Add Details'.

All B2B invoice details are to be entered under this tab.

Click on the relevant field, i.e., whether it is deemed exports, SEZ supplies, etc.

Fill in other details of the invoice.

Click 'Save', once all details of an invoice are entered.

Note: The data from E-way bills can be directly imported from the EWB system by clicking 'Import EWB Data'.

FIGURE 5.16

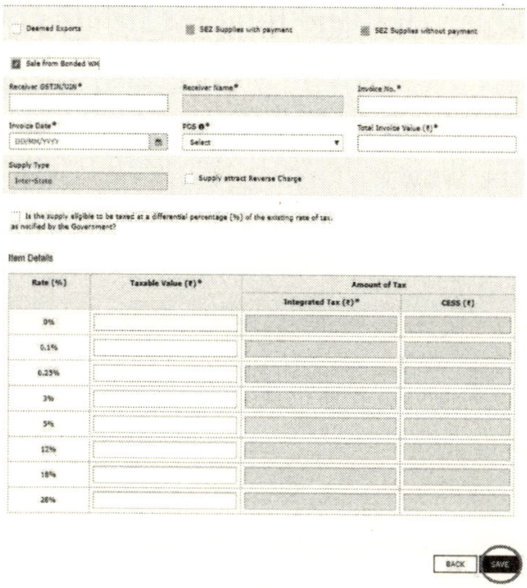

Step 9: Click 'Add Details' to add more invoices.

A summary of all invoices entered will be displayed. The invoices can be 'Edited/Deleted' under the 'Actions' column.

Click 'Back' to go back to the 'Invoices – Receiver-Wise-Summary' page. To add more invoices of a particular receiver, click on the particular receiver and 'Add Invoice'.

Click 'Back' to go to the main page.

B2B tab would now reflect the total invoice value, total taxable value, and total tax liability.

All other tabs are to be filled with relevant details in the same way.

FIGURE 5.17

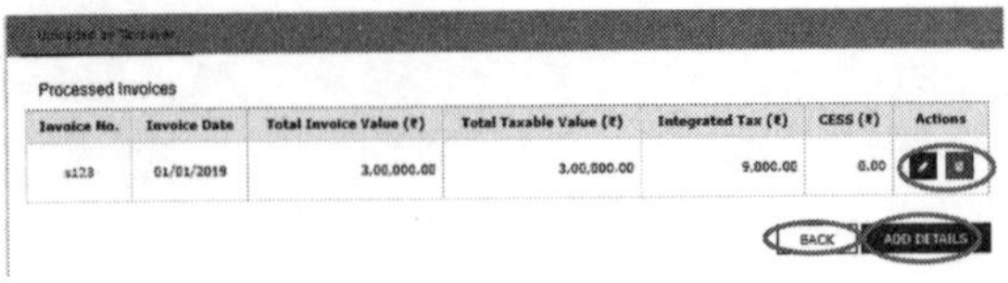

Step 10: After all the relevant details are filled in all the tabs, click 'Generate GSTR1 Summary'.

Once the summary return is reviewed, any changes to be made in any tabs should be done at this stage by reopening the tabs and filling in the correct data. Click on 'Acknowledgment' > 'Submit' > 'Proceed'. Once the return is submitted, no changes can be made in the return.

Click 'File Return' > 'File with EVC/DSC' > 'Proceed'. The return is then filed.

FIGURE 5.18

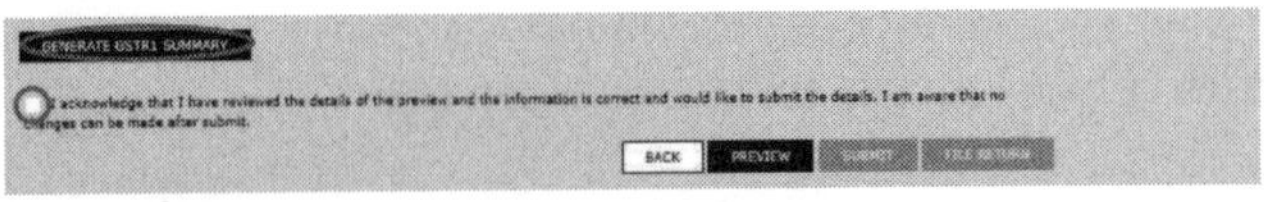

It is to be noted that other returns are to be filed in a similar manner.

It is important to note here that Government has come up with a new return format which is a simplified return form. The new format has been introduced and is available on the GSTN portal for trial run. The taxpayers can fill in their data on the new trial version and can suggest any improvements in the return form to the Government.

Under the new return formats, the threshold for quarterly filing of return has been increased from 1.5 crores to 5 crores. It also provides for revision/ amendment of return already filed, which is not present under the existing return filing system. Multiple return forms for various categories of taxpayers has been done away with and three new forms have been introduced, viz.: GST Return (Normal), GST Return (Sahaj), GST Return (Sugam). The taxpayer can choose which return form he has to file based on the kind of transactions he has. The new return forms may be applicable from April 2020 or such further date notified by the Government.

Okay, and how can one pay taxes?

Taxes can be paid in the following manner:

Step 1: Login to www.gst.gov.in.
Step 2: Go to 'Services' > 'Payments' > 'Create Challan'.

FIGURE 5.19

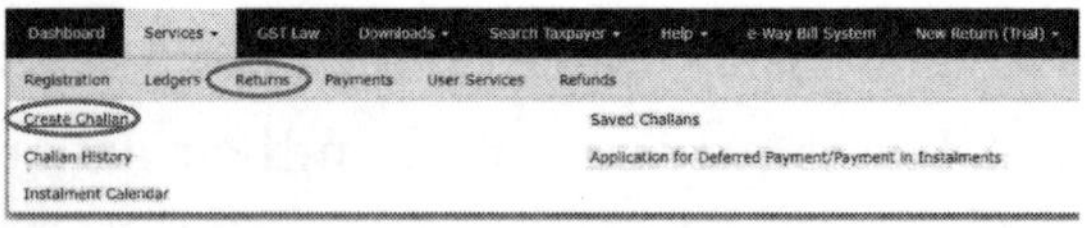

Step 3: Enter the tax amount under the appropriate tax head (i.e., CGST & SGST or IGST). Any interest, penalty or fees if any, also needs to be entered.

Select the payment mode through which GST would be paid.

Click 'Generate Challan'

FIGURE 5.20

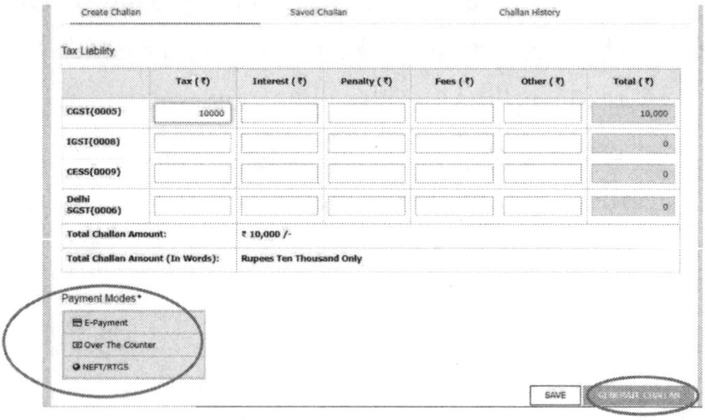

Step 4: Challan would be generated.

Select the mode of payment and click 'Make Payment'.

Click 'Proceed'.

Tax payment would be made.

FIGURE 5.21

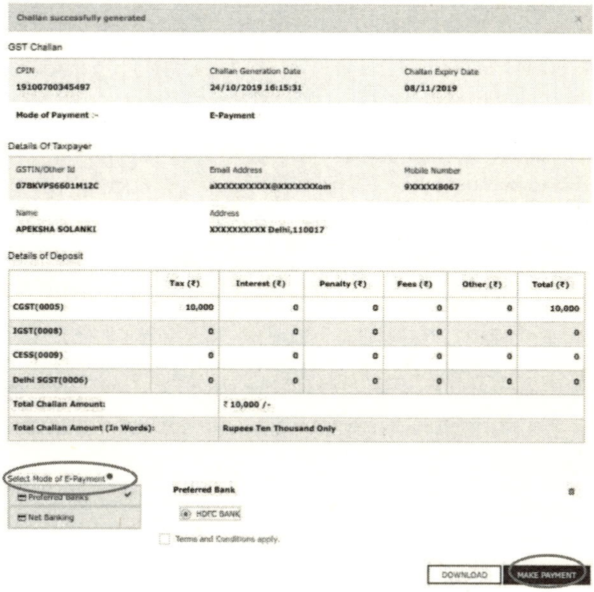

Assessment, Audit and Appeals

GG, what does assessment mean under GST law?

Assessment

Assessment implies the determination of tax liability of a person. A taxpayer would know how much tax he has to pay on a regular and continuous basis only after assessment. The two major factors required to determine tax liability are the tax rate and the value of supply. However, since calculating those two factors may need a lot of deliberation and time, it is not always easy to calculate tax liability.

There are various types of assessments under GST:

FIGURE 6.1

Self Assessment

- The registered person is required to assesss the tax liability on his/her own, without interevention of any tax officer and accordingly pay the taxes and file returns within the prescribed time limit

Provisional Assessment

- In case the taxpayer finds it difficult to determine his/her own tax liability (i.e., undertake self assessment) then he can furnish an application to the tax officer for provisional assessment and pay the taxes on a provisional basis
- Provisional Assessment has to be initiated by the taxpayer himself herself and not by the tax officer
- The tax officer, on receipt of application, may ask for further information and pass the final order within the prescribed time limit
- Once the final order is passed, the taxpayer may have to pay extra tax along with interest, if he/she had paid less tax on provisional basis—or he/she may get a refund along with interest, if he/she had paid more tax on provisional basis

Best Judgement Assessment (BJA)

- In case of non-filers of return
  - Where a taxpayer has failed to file the return even after receiving a notice for doing so by the tax officer, the tax officer can undertake Best Judgment Assessment. It is an assessment inititated by the tax officer on his/her own
  - Under BJA, the tax officer passes the order, to the best of his/her judgment basis, all the relevant materials gathered by him/her or available to him/her about the taxpayer
- In case of an unregistered person, where the person is liable to take registration under GST Act
  - The final order under BJA can be passed by the tax officer only after giving a notice and an opportunity of being heard to the taxpayer.
- BJA order can be passed by the tax officer within a period of five years from the due date of furnishing the annual return to which the tax not paid relates

Summary Assessment (SA)/ Protective Assessment

- It is an exceptional power given to the tax officer and can be initiated only with prior permission of Additional Commissioner or Joint Commissioner
- A tax officer can go ahead with SA only to protect the interest of the government, provided he/she has sufficient grounds to belive that any delay in passing the assessment order is likely to affect the interest of revenue

Okay, and what happens once the assessee files his/her return of income?

Scrutiny of Returns

Under GST, taxpayers are required to self-assess their tax liability and then file the returns. Since GST is a trust-based regime, it is important to have a robust mechanism in place to ensure that compliance with law has taken place. Therefore, once the returns have been filed, the tax officers select a few returns on basis of materiality and scrutinise them for their accuracy and compliance with the law. Any discrepancies found are communicated by issuing a notice to the taxpayer.

The taxpayer is required to reply to the notice within the prescribed time limit. If the reply is found to be acceptable or if the taxpayer has accepted the discrepancies pointed out in the notice, the tax officer takes no further action. However, if the reply is not found to be acceptable, the tax officer may undertake any of the below activities:

1. Conduct audit of the taxpayer.
2. Direct a special audit to be conducted by a chartered accountant or cost accountant.

3. Undertake inspection, search and seizure.
4. Initiate proceedings for issue of show-cause notice and adjudication thereof.

FIGURE 6.2

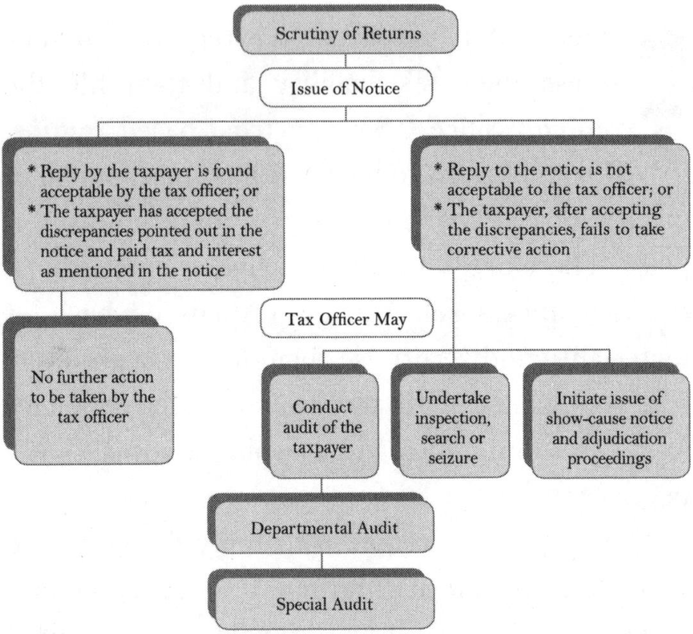

Can you explain a bit about the actions that a tax officer may take?

Sure, let me briefly explain them to you.

1. *Audit*: Audit means to examine records and other documents maintained by the

taxpayer to verify the correctness of turnover declared, taxes paid and other particulars declared in the return and to assess compliance with the provisions of GST law.

Audit can be of two types:

(a) Departmental Audit: The tax officer can undertake audit of a registered person, for any financial year at such frequency and in such manner as may be prescribed by the law. Tax officers normally visit the taxpayer's business premises for conduct of audit. Tax department has developed various risk parameters for selection of taxpayers for audit based upon risk quantification.

(b) Special Audit: If, at any stage of scrutiny, inquiry, investigation or any other proceedings before the revenue authorities, the tax officer feels that because of the complexity of the case and in the interest of the revenue, it is necessary that the books of accounts and records of the taxpayer gets audited by a chartered accountant or a cost accountant, then he may direct the taxpayer to do so. In this case, the cost of a chartered accountant or a cost accountant is to be borne by the revenue authorities.

2. *Inspection*: GST law provides for inspection by a tax officer which enables him/her to access any place of business of a taxpayer, where he/she has reasons to believe that the taxpayer has not reported any transaction related to supply of goods or services or stock of goods in hand or has claimed excess input tax credit or has contravened any other provisions of the law.
3. *Search and Seizure*: Where a tax officer, on the basis of inspection or otherwise, has reasons to believe that any goods or relevant documents of a taxpayer, liable to confiscation, are hidden in any place, may search any premise and seize the goods or documents.
4. *Adjudication Proceedings*: Where the tax officer finds that tax has been short-paid or input tax credit has been wrongly availed or utilised, he/she may issue a show-cause notice (SCN) to the taxpayer, requiring him/her to show cause as to why the latter should not pay the tax along with interest and/or penalty as mentioned in the notice.

Normally, when adjudication proceedings take place, the following steps, shown in Figure 6.3, are taken:

FIGURE 6.3

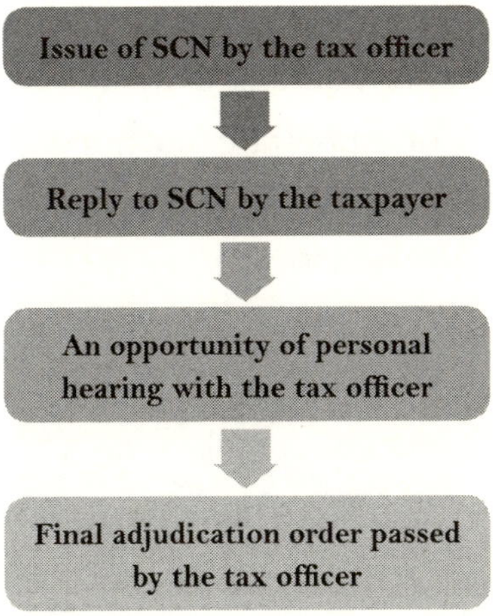

And what happens if the taxpayer does not agree with the order of the adjudicating authority?

Appeals

It is possible that the taxpayer does not agree with the order passed by the adjudicating authority. It is also possible that the Department itself (i.e. revenue authorities) may not agree with the adjudication order. In such cases, both the taxpayer and the Department have a solution—which is to appeal to a higher authority against the order passed by the lower authority.

The law provides four levels of appeal if the aggrieved person (i.e., the tax payer or the Department) is not satisfied with the order passed at each level of appellate authority. The appeal process that can be followed by the aggrieved party is shown in Figure 6.4:

FIGURE 6.4

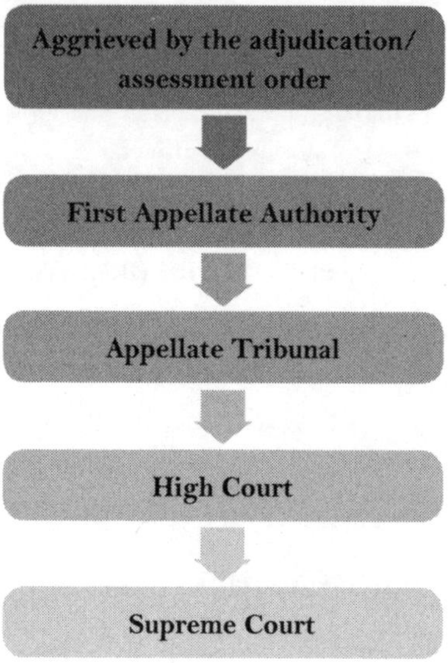

Important points to keep in mind before filing an appeal at any level:

1. Since India has a dual GST model, i.e. every transaction attracts both CGST and

SGST, it is not required that appeal be filed separately before both CGST and SGST authorities. Cross empowerment between CGST and SGST officers is provided, which ensures that an order passed by an officer, under one Act, will hold good for both the CGST and SGST component of the same transaction.

2. Appeal to the next higher authority should be filed within the prescribed time limit and is admitted only after payment of prescribed fee.
3. Appeal can be filed electronically on the GST portal or physically at the government office.
4. Opportunity of hearing is always given to both the parties before the final order is passed by the authority. Also, the authorities may grant time and adjourn the hearing to the parties if they so require. However, not more than three adjournments are granted.
5. If, in any case, the dispute pertains to facts of the case, then an Appellate Tribunal is the last fact finding authority. An appeal to a high court or the Supreme Court can be admitted only if the case involves substantial questions of law.

People's Response to GST

Thank you, GG, for so much gyan on GST. Having learnt so much about it, I feel like, while there may be a lot of advantages to its introduction, there must also be a few shortcomings. You must have observed people's reactions to it—why don't you share some of those experiences with us?

Sure, why not? The introduction of GST has garnered mixed reactions from consumers and industry. As is true with any new change, GST has brought about a lot of commendation as well as criticisms. Some of the reactions have been enumerated below.

Commendation of GST

1. *Subsuming of Many Indirect Taxes into GST:* A lot of indirect taxes levied by the Central government and state governments have been subsumed into GST. Many taxes were

levied on the same goods at different stage in consumer chain. The subsuming of such taxes into one has resulted in simplification of the tax system and reduced compliances.

2. *Reduction of Net Tax Incidence on Consumer:* On the face of it, GST rates may seem higher than the rates of excise duty or service tax or VAT, which were prevalent in the erstwhile regime. However, earlier, a lot of indirect taxes were levied throughout the consumer chain which were not visible to the end consumer; complete credit of those taxes was also not available. Under GST—even though the tax rates appear higher—in almost all cases, the net tax rate has reduced as compared to the total of all indirect taxes levied on the same goods or services in the pre-GST regime.
3. *Elimination of Cascading Effect of Taxes:* One of the biggest victories of the introduction of GST has been the elimination of tax on tax. Under the pre-GST regime, taxes paid to the state government were not eligible for input tax credit against liability under Central taxes— and vice-versa. For example, excise duty, or service tax paid, were not allowed credit against the liability of VAT. In GST, as only one tax, i.e. GST,

is paid for the entire transaction chain, it is allowed credit for liability against the next stage. This has led to substantial reduction in the tax burden for end consumers.

4. *Abolition of CST and India Becoming One Common Market:* In the pre-GST era, CST levied by the originating state for inter-state movement of goods was not available as tax credit to the dealer in the receiving state, resulting in CST becoming a part of the cost of the product. Under the GST regime, however, the IGST paid in the originating state is fully available as credit to a dealer in the recipient state. This has made India one common market and has increased the economic activity across the states.
5. *Transparency to End Consumers:* Since just one tax is levied throughout the consumer chain, customers are aware of the actual tax that they are paying. In the erstwhile regime, a lot of taxes formed part of the cost of the product, like excise duty, octroi, etc., and some of them were not visible to the end consumers. To illustrate, a car buyer was never aware that he paid excise duty, service tax and CST—none of which could be seen in the invoice, even though they possibly formed up to 25–30% of the cost of the car.

6. *One Tax, Simpler Tax:* It is easier to keep track of the provisions of one tax rather than to keep track of various taxes. Earlier, provisions of various laws like excise, service tax, VAT, CST, entry tax, etc. had to be kept abreast with. With just one tax now, companies don't need to devote a lot of resources to just tax compliances. Moreover, entities with a multi-state presence needed to know the VAT laws of each state, which were very complex in nature.
7. *Efficient Logistics:* In the earlier regime, the movement of goods across state borders led to a delay in shipments because of state-border checkposts. Introduction of IGST and removal of border checkposts has been one of the biggest advantages under GST, as goods can now cross state borders without any trouble from tax authorities. It has also led to a substantial increase in the efficiency of the transportation sector, leading to reduction in freight cost.
8. *Strong Tracking System:* Every GST compliance (like registration, filing of returns, etc.) is done through GSTN, which renders every piece of information about a taxpayer easily available online. The advantage of making a network that strong and well-connected

is that it is hard to miss out on any vital information since everything is linked on GSTN. For example, if a taxpayer has missed accounting for a purchase bill in the books of account, he will still not miss the input tax credit available on such purchases as his/her vendor would have shown that as sales in the GSTR-1 return filed by him/her—which would be auto populated as purchases in GSTR-2A of the taxpayer.

9. *Simplification of Indirect Tax Laws:* The GST structure itself has removed many inherent disputes prevalent in erstwhile laws. Taxability of composite contract under works contract system is one such area, where both the Central as well as state governments were levying taxes, leading to perennial disputes. This has now been resolved as only one tax is being levied on such a transaction. Yet another example is that of taxes on software. In the earlier regime, there were demands for payment of customs duty, service tax and VAT on the same transaction of import/further sale of software. It was treated as import of service by the service tax authorities and import of goods by the customs authority, leading to levy of customs duty—as well as service

tax—on the same activity. Under GST, if software is imported as goods, only customs duty is payable. However, if it is treated as services, only GST would be payable and there would be no dual demand for customs duty *and* service tax.

10. *Option to File Return Quarterly:* Small taxpayers with a turnover of up to ₹1.5 crore can file a quarterly return, along with monthly payment of taxes. This facility is optional, which means that the taxpayer can choose to file monthly returns also.

Criticisms of GST

1. *Higher Compliance Burden:* GST has invited the most criticism for the substantial increase of compliance burden. Under GST, the detail of each sales invoice is required to be entered in the return. Moreover, these details also need to be matched with what the supplier has entered in his/her return in order to avail input tax credit. There are also other minute details that need to be declared by a taxpayer such as, declaring each item sent for job work, annual return, reconciliation statement, etc.—all of which have added to taxpayer woes. These details

need to be entered online on the GSTN portal. The worst sufferers are small and medium taxpayers who are not computer savvy and have to spend substantial amounts on compliance fulfilment. Also, there is a general fear about incorrect feeding of data in the return which cannot be revised.

2. *Cash Flow Problems:* Under GST, a lot of small or new businesses are facing a liquidity crunch. This working capital shortage is caused due to various reasons:
   (a) The liability to pay GST, even for a partnership firm or a sole proprietorship, is monthly—whereas under the service tax regime, tax was to be deposited quarterly. This has created an adverse effect on the liquidity as tax remittance has been changed to a monthly cycle.
   (b) Rate of GST for services has increased from 15% to 18%. This would also lead to increase in need of funds to discharge the tax liability.
   (c) Delay in processing of refunds to exporters also affects the cash flow requirements.
   (d) Applicability of TCS provisions under GST regime on all e-commerce transactions

also has an adverse effect on cash flow requirements.

3. *Frequent Changes in Law:* There have been frequent changes in the GST law and procedure. Even tax practitioners are finding it difficult to keep track of all the changes that have been made by the government ever since GST was first introduced. Further, the government has not provided any amnesty during GST's initial period to waive interest and penalty for genuine lapses due to unintentional irregularities.
4. *No Special Benefit Given to New Businesses/ Start-ups:* India is the third largest start-up ecosystem around the globe. While the government harps on 'Make in India', no special benefits are accorded to start-ups or freelancers, under GST. All rules applicable under GST to a particular industry are also applicable to a start-up in that particular industry.
5. *Lower Threshold Limit for Manufacturing Units:* Under the erstwhile tax regime, manufacturing units with a turnover of less than ₹1.5 crore did not have to be registered under excise law. However, under GST, the threshold has been drastically reduced to

₹40 lakh, bringing in many small businesses under the tax net.

6. *Credit of Input Tax Dependent on Vendor:* Input tax credit would be available to a buyer only when his/her vendor deposits GST with the government and files the details of tax paid in his/her return. For example, Ms S sells goods to Ms B. The buyer, Ms B, can take credit of input tax in her return only when Ms S deposits GST with the government and uploads the details of sales in her return in form GSTR-1. If the seller fails to deposit the tax paid by the buyer with the government—or does not file her return in time—then the purchaser cannot claim input tax credit of GST paid by her, even though she has paid tax to the seller. This is a double whammy for a buyer.
7. *System-related GSTN Issues:* A lot of technical issues still persist with the online GST portal. A lot of bugs and faults while filing the return or other compliance forms still exist. This is time consuming.
8. *No Provision to Revise GST Return:* GST law has no provision to revise the return once it has been filed. This provision is very harsh, as so many times after filing the return, the taxpayers realise that they

have inadvertently missed out on some information or put in wrong information. For example, a person may erroneously show input tax credit in his/her return as ₹12,755,000 instead of 127,550 (possibly missing the '.'). This may lead to a situation where the tax department may demand interest on wrongly availed credit, even though the taxpayer may not have utilised said credit. Hence, there should be a provision to revise returns. However, the government paid heed to this grievance and has provided for amendment of returns in the new GST return format which will be introduced soon.

9. *E-commerce Aggregators to Collect Tax Collected at Source (TCS):* E-commerce aggregators like Flipkart, Swiggy, etc. have to collect TCS from payments received on behalf of dealers associated with them on their platform. TCS so collected has to be deposited with the government and the net balance payment after deduction of TCS is paid to the dealers. This has increased a lot of compliance burden for such aggregators. For example, it is well known that Flipkart has a lot of sellers registered on its platform. It receives payment from buyers which it

passes on to the sellers. However, when Flipkart makes payments to its sellers, it will have to first deduct TCS and deposit it with the government and then pay the balance amount (net of TCS) to the sellers.

10. *Deeming Transaction Between Branches/ Offices in Two Different States:* As per GST law, if a business has branches/offices in two different states, then such branches/offices are treated as separate legal persons and any transaction between them is liable to tax. This has resulted in many unwarranted compliances. Essentially, any service availed by the head office for all the offices across the country are deemed to be for providing services to offices in other states—which require cross-charge of expenses on payment of GST.
11. *Revenue-biased Rulings by Authority for Advanced Ruling (AAR):* It has been a common observation by most people that rulings issued by the AAR are generally revenue-biased. One of the reasons is that the members of AAR are junior-ranked tax officers. This problem can be solved if AAR members are officers from judicial backgrounds and/or are senior tax officers.

PART B

WHAT'S IN IT FOR ME?

Monday Blues Are Not for Me: GST for Salaried Employees

GG, would GST have any impact on my salary structure? GST is levied on supply of goods and services, so as an employee, do my services to the employer attract GST?

GST law specifically states that services provided by an employee to his/her employer in the course of his/her employment is outside the ambit of GST. So any services provided by an employee, in terms of the employment contract, will not be liable to GST.

However, there may be different components of the salary or other payments received by an employee, which may have different treatments under GST. We can see them in detail in Table 8.1:

TABLE 8.1

Sl. No.	Payments Received by an Employee	Treatment under GST
1.	Salary paid to employees	Services by an employee to his/her employer in the course of his/her employment is specifically kept out of the ambit of GST. Hence, GST is not applicable on salary paid to employees
	Fee paid for services provided, other than those specified in the employment contract	Any service provided by an employee outside the scope of employment contract would attract GST. For example, an IT professional gives dance lessons to her employer after office hours. Since the scope of employment agreement would be restricted to IT-related office work, the fee paid for dance lessons will be liable to GST *(provided the total value of dance service provided by the employee crosses the threshold limit of ₹20 lakh)*
2.	Bonus or other incentives (like relocation benefits, long services awards, staff reference fee, etc.) paid to employees	Incentives are generally paid in relation to employment. Therefore, GST is not applicable on bonus or incentives paid

Sl. No.	Payments Received by an Employee	Treatment under GST
3.	Payments made to directors of a company:	
	Whole-time director or an executive director	They are generally regarded as employees of the company. Hence, payment made to them as salary is made in the course of employment and will not be liable to GST
	Independent directors/ nominee director/ non-executive directors	They are not regarded as employees of the company. Hence, payment made to them (commonly known as director's fee or board meeting fee or sitting fee) for their services to the company will be liable to GST. *(It must be noted here that the company has to pay GST on behalf of the directors under reverse charge mechanism)*
4.	Contract employees or freelancers	They work on principal-to-principal basis and not in the course of employment.Therefore, GST is applicable on payments made to contract employees or freelancers
5.	Stipend paid to interns	There exists an employer-employee relationship between interns and their employer. Services provided in the course of employment are out of the ambit of GST. Therefore, GST is not applicable on stipends paid to interns
6.	Payment made to employee for premature termination of employment contract	Such payment is made in the course of employment and, hence, will not be liable to GST

»

Sl. No.	Payments Received by an Employee	Treatment under GST
7.	Non-competing fee	Any fee paid for not joining a competing business for a particular period would be liable to GST as such payment is not made in the course of employment
8.	Canteen expenses recovered from employees	In a recent ruling by Authority for Advance Ruling, it was held that food provided by employers to employees qualifies as services provided and, hence, GST would be applicable
9.	Membership of clubs or fitness centres or health centres	Where as per the employment contract such services are provided to employees free of cost, then no GST is applicable, provided GST is paid by employer on procurement of these services. These services become part of cost-to-company (CTC) and hence not taxable
10.	Other perquisites provided to employees (like transport allowance, uniform allowance, etc.)	Perquisites are provided for in the employment contract and form part of the CTC. Therefore, GST is not applicable on perquisites given to employees
11.	Gifts given to employees by their employer	Gifts, not exceeding ₹50,000 in value given in a financial year, do not attract GST. However, gifts of value of more than ₹50,000 given in a financial year will be subject to GST. For example, any ex-gratia payment, like a Diwali gift is not part of the employment contract and, hence, considered a gift. But, uniforms given to employees are part of the employment contract and hence, would not be considered as gift

Sl. No.	Payments Received by an Employee	Treatment under GST
12.	Free housing to employee	When house is provided free of cost as per terms of employment contract, GST will not be applicable as it becomes part of CTC
	Renting of house to employees	In a case where the company provides a house to an employee for his/her residence, on rent, and deducts the rent from his/her salary, GST is not applicable on the rent so deducted because house given on rent for residential purposes is specifically kept out of the ambit of GST
13.	Sale of used assets to employees like laptops, cars, furniture, etc.	GST would be applicable as the same would qualify as supply of goods
	Sale of products at concessional rate	GST would be applicable on the fair market value of the product. GST law states that where two related parties transact, GST would be applicable at fair market value of the product. It also states that the relationship between employer and employee is that of a related person. Therefore, any product provided to an employee at concessional rate would be taxed at the fair market value of the goods. For example, a cosmetic company provides 40% discount to all its employees for purchase of cosmetics from the company. Say, a lipstick costs ₹100, but the employee has to pay only ₹60 for it. However, GST would be calculated on the fair market value of the product, i.e. GST would be calculated on ₹100 and not on ₹60

»

Sl. No.	Payments Received by an Employee	Treatment under GST
14.	Contribution towards provident fund scheme	No GST is applicable on contribution towards any provident fund scheme
	Services provided by Employees Provident Fund Organisation (EPFO)	Any fee charged for service provided (like administration charges) by EPFO to its members is specifically kept out of the ambit of GST. However, fee for service provided by any other provident fund, other than EPFO, would be liable to GST
15.	Contribution towards National Pension System Trust (NPS)	No GST is applicable on contribution towards NPS scheme
	Services provided by NPS	Services (like administration fee, etc.) provided by NPS to its members is specifically kept out of the ambit of GST
16.	Professional tax	Professional tax is a state levy and is imposed by very few state governments in India (like Maharashtra). It is a tax levied on income earned by salaried employees and professionals, including chartered accountants, lawyers, etc. Professional tax is not levied on supply of goods and services. It is not subsumed under GST, and continues to be levied by select state governments

GST on Banking, Insurance and Financial Services

How has GST impacted the various financial and banking services availed by someone in his/her daily life?

GST on Banking and Financial Services

Under the service tax regime, tax on financial services (like a few referred to in Table 9.1) was levied at the rate of 15%. Under GST, all financial services are levied at 18%, making them marginally costlier. This increase in the rate of tax would, however, be neutralised by availability of additional input credits of GST paid on goods, including capital goods used by banks (earlier VAT was applicable on goods and, hence, credit against the output service tax liability of banks was not available).

The impact of GST on various banking and financial services is discussed in Table 9.1.

TABLE 9.1

Sl. No.	Scenarios	Treatment under GST
1.	Cash withdrawals from ATM:	
	Up to free number of cash withdrawals allowed	Services provided free of cost do not attract GST, unless they are provided to a related party. Therefore, cash withdrawals from an ATM up to the free number of withdrawals allowed do not attract GST
	Beyond the specified number of free withdrawals allowed	Banks charge a transaction fee from customers if they withdraw money from an ATM beyond the allowed free limit. GST is applicable on such fee charged by the banks
2.	Free services provided by banks like issuance of cheque book, mini statements, ATM PIN change, etc.	As per GST law, any supply provided to unrelated parties without any consideration does not attract GST. Therefore, free services provided by banks do not attract GST

Sl. No.	Scenarios	Treatment under GST
3.	Debit and credit card services :	
	Annual fee charged for debit or credit cards	Annual fee charged by banks to customers is subject to GST
	Late payment charges for outstanding credit card bill	GST is applicable on late fee charged by banks for delayed payment of credit card dues
	Fee charged for replacement of lost or damaged card	If the banks charge fee for replacement of cards, then GST is applicable on such fee
	Lounge facilities on credit cards	Any lounge access fee charged, beyond the complimentary access, would be subject to GST
4.	Money transfer services: Services offered by banks for instant money transfer through electronic mode, like transfer through NEFT/ RTGS/IMPS mode	Banks charge transaction fee or internet banking charges for providing such services. GST is applicable on these financial services offered by banks
5.	Issuance of Demand Draft (DD)	Transactions involving instruments like cheque, demand drafts, pay orders, promissory note, letters of credit, etc. are outside the ambit of GST. Therefore, issuance of DD will not attract GST. However, any service charges/administrative fee charged by a bank to a customer to issue DD or any of the above-mentioned instruments would be liable to GST

»

Sl. No.	Scenarios	Treatment under GST
6.	Loans/ deposits/ advances (where the consideration is time value of money and is paid by way of interest or through discounting):	Money borrowed is a transaction in money. Money is neither supply of goods nor services, hence, GST is not applicable
	Interest on loan	Interest on loan is specifically kept out of the ambit of GST. Hence, GST is not applicable
	Default in payment of interest	Any additional interest charged by a bank for delay in payment of interest on loan is not liable to GST
	Loan processing fee or service charges or administrative charges for processing of loans or advances or deposits	GST is applicable on such charges
	Invoice discounting/ cheque discounting	Discounting is a manner of extending loan or credit facility where the consideration is paid by way of discounting. Therefore, GST is not applicable
7.	Fixed deposits/ savings bank deposits/other bank deposits on which return is received by way of interest	It is specifically kept out of the ambit of GST. Hence, GST is not applicable
8.	Sale of repossessed assets by banks	Such sale comes within the scope of supply of goods, hence, GST is applicable

Sl. No.	Scenarios	Treatment under GST
9.	Overdraft facility/ credit limit facility, consideration for which is paid by way of interest	Any advances for which consideration is paid by way of interest does not attract GST. Hence, GST is not applicable
10.	Wealth Management Services:	
	Mutual fund services	Fee charged for managing the fund (fund management services) attracts GST
	Exit load charged by mutual funds	Exit load charged for opting out of a mutual fund scheme earlier than the stipulated time in the contract attracts GST
	Purchase and sale of securities like shares/ stocks/bonds	Purchase and sale of securities is neither supply of goods nor services, therefore, it does not attract GST. However, any service charges or fee that may be charged to facilitate such purchase or sale attracts GST
	Interest on debt instruments like debentures, bonds, etc.	Debt instruments are in the nature of loans, therefore, interest on them will not attract GST
	Stock broking services/services of mutual fund distributors/services of investment advisor or investment planner or financial advisor	GST is applicable on all such services

»

»

Sl. No.	Scenarios	Treatment under GST
11.	Safe deposit locker charges	Fee charged for availing services of safe deposit lockers in banks attracts GST

For all the transactions mentioned in Table 9.1, bank can issue a consolidated bill to a customer for all transactions undertaken during a month on which GST has been charged. If customer is using these services for his/her business, he/she can give his/her GST registration number to the bank, so that the latter can issue a taxable invoice, basing which the customer can avail credit of GST paid on the said financial services.

How about the impact of GST on insurance services?

GST on Insurance Services

Any person who enjoys insurance services, has to pay insurance premium as a consideration for such services. Insurance premiums are subject to indirect taxes. Under GST, the cost of insurance premiums has also marginally increased, as the tax rate has increased from 15% under service tax regime to 18% under GST regime. Whether life insurance or general insurance services (like fire insurance, car insurance, theft insurance, health insurance, etc.), these are all affected by GST. However, a few specified life and general insurance schemes provided by the government are specifically exempt from tax.

It is pertinent to note here that, in case of a life insurance policy, the taxable value of supply of services for GST depends on the type of insurance policy. The following methods may be applied to determine the value of supply, in case of a life insurance policy that is taxable under GST:

#DIY_tip

1. *Term Policies*: Where the entire premium is paid towards life risk cover only, taxable value is the entire premium (i.e. 100% of premium) charged from the policy holder.
2. *Endowment Policies/Unit Link Insurance Policies:* Where an insurance policy has dual benefits of risk coverage and investment, taxable value is the gross premium charged minus the amount allocated for investments. This method of calculation can be used only if the amount allocated for investments is

intimated to the policy holder at the time of collection of premium, like in the case of ULIP.

3. *Single Premium Annuity Policies*: The taxable value is 10% of the premium charged from the policy holder. In this case, allocation for investments is not communicated to the policy holder.
4. *Other Policies:* Taxable value for the first year would be 25% of the premium charged and for subsequent years it would be 12.5% of the premium charged. It is important to note that individuals who take life or health insurance services (from their work organisation or otherwise) do not have the benefit of input tax credit as these are for personal consumption. However, a corporate can avail benefit of input tax credit on premium paid by them on general insurance (such as theft or fire) services taken by them. But, where a corporate has taken life or health insurance policy for its employees, it is not eligible for input tax credit, unless the requirement to take insurance is obligatory under any other Indian law.
5. *Policies for NRIs:* Also, life insurance policies issued to Non-Resident Indians

(NRIs), where insurance premium is paid through Non-Resident External Accounts, are not treated as exports, as payments are received in Indian rupees and not in convertible foreign exchange. Therefore, GST would be applicable on premium paid by such NRIs.

Okay, and how about treatment of purchase and sale of foreign currency by an individual?

GST on Purchase and Sale of Foreign Currency

Purchase and sale of foreign currency by an individual or foreign exchange services also attract GST. Government has provided for specific rules to determine the value on which GST is applicable in such cases:

1. For a currency when exchanged from or to INR:
   (a) Purchase of foreign currency by service supplier:
   Taxable value (on which GST would be applicable) = Buying rate* x total units of currency

(b) Sale of foreign currency by service supplier:
Taxable value = Selling rate* x total units of currency
**RBI reference rate at that time is taken. If RBI reference rate is not available, then taxable value would be 1% of the gross amount of INR provided or received by the person changing the money.*

2. The supplier of service also has an option to use the following method, as shown in Table 9.2, for valuation of service in relation to supply of foreign currency:

TABLE 9.2

For an Amount	Value of Supply Shall be Calculated at
Up to ₹1 lakh	1% of gross amount of currency exchanged; or ₹250, whichever is higher
₹1 lakh to ₹10 lakh	₹1,000 + 0.5% of gross amount of currency exchanged
Exceeding ₹10 lakh	₹5,500 + 0.1% of gross amount of currency exchanged; or ₹60,000, whichever is lower

Note: This option once availed, cannot be withdrawn during the remaining part of the financial year.

The Kirana Shop: GST for Small Businesses

Hello, Baniyaji, why do you look so worried?

This GST has caused so much trouble! I don't know how I am going to manage my shop. I fear, I may just have to shut down my business! What am I going to do now?

But why would you have to shut down your business?

Well, because GST does not seem very friendly for small businesses like mine. The GST rates are so high. Moreover, I have even heard that it would be necessary for all to take GST registration, because people would not prefer transacting with unregistered dealers. Also, the number of returns and other compliances under

GST has increased manifold. The process of preparing and filing returns has become much more complicated. Moreover, everything has moved online, and a small business person like me is not well versed with computers and the internet. How will I be able to manage all this?

Oh my God! Your worries are totally unnecessary. GST law has lenient provisions for small businesses like yours.

Like what?

The first and foremost is that, if a person has a turnover of goods of less than ₹40 lakh in a financial year and if he does not deal in inter-state supplies, then he need not register under GST.

Second, GST also has composition scheme which is an alternative method of levy of tax for small taxpayers. According to this scheme, tax has to be paid at a concessional rate on the total turnover of the taxpayer. This eliminates the need to maintain detailed accounts and records. The amount of compliance required under composition scheme is also much less as compared to regular tax payment scheme.

The basic objective of composition scheme is to make things simple and reduce the cost of compliance for small taxpayers. It is a voluntary and optional tax payment scheme.

Hmm, so who exactly can opt for a composition scheme?

A registered person dealing in goods whose aggregate turnover in the preceding financial year did not exceed ₹1.5 crore will be eligible to opt for composition scheme in the current year. The said limit of aggregate turnover would be ₹75 lakh for Special Category states—Arunachal Pradesh, Assam, Manipur, Meghalaya, Mizoram, Nagaland, Sikkim, Tripura and Uttrakhand. However, for a service provider (a person who provides only services), the threshold limit is ₹50 lakh.

Also, a supplier of goods who also provides services is permitted to avail the scheme, if the value of supply of services is

1. Up to 10% of his/her turnover in a state; or
2. Up to ₹5 lakh,

whichever is higher.

For example, a trader in goods, who is earning commission income or service income (i.e. he/she is providing services) upto the above mentioned prescribed limit, will be allowed to avail composition scheme.

Can you help me with calculating my aggregate turnover, so that I know whether I am eligible for composition scheme or not?

Calculation of aggregate turnover is very simple. It is the sum total of turnover of all business entities across India registered on the same PAN. A person may calculate their aggregate turnover by doing a sum total of:

1. All supplies which are taxable under GST law.
2. All supplies of goods and services which are exempt under GST law.
3. Exports of goods and/or services.
4. All inter-state supplies.

   However, while calculating aggregate turnover, the following items should not be included:

   1. Value of all purchases on which tax was paid on reverse charge basis.

2. All taxes, including cess paid under GST law (like CGST, SGST, IGST, UGST).
3. Any interest income on loans or advances made by a person.

On the basis of the aggregate turnover calculated above, for the previous year, you can decide whether you are eligible for composition scheme in the current year.

This seems like something that I can calculate on my own. And at what rates do I have to pay tax under the composition scheme?

Tax rates applicable under composition scheme can be seen in Table 10.1:

TABLE 10.1

Type of Business	CGST	SGST	Total Rate of GST	Conditions
Manufacturer	0.5%	0.5%	1%	1% of turnover in state or union territory *(which means that tax is payable even on supplies which are otherwise exempt from GST)**

Type of Business	CGST	SGST	Total Rate of GST	Conditions
Traders	0.5%	0.5%	1%	1% of turnover of taxable supplies in a state or UT *(which means tax is not to be paid on exempt supplies)**
Service Providers	3%	3%	6%	6 % of turnover in state or UT *(which means that tax is payable even on supplies which are otherwise exempt from GST)**
Restaurants	2.5%	2.5%	5%	5% of turnover in state or UT *(which means that tax is payable even on supplies which are otherwise exempt from GST)**

**Note: GST is not payable on interest income earned on extending loan or advances.*

#GG_tip

Table 10.1 clearly shows that, in case of manufacturers or service providers, including restaurant service providers, who provide both exempt and taxable goods, tax under composition scheme is payable even on exempted goods and services, excluding on interest income on extending loan and advances. Such persons can consider supplying exempted goods and services under a different company/firm (which has a different PAN) to avoid tax on exempted goods and services.

Okay, so now I can go ahead and pay my taxes as per composition scheme.

Yes, you can. But you have to be careful that you do not fall in the category of people who are not eligible for the composition scheme (*as seen in Figure 10.1*):

FIGURE 10.1

- Person supplying goods which are not taxable under GST law
- Person supplying goods through electronic commerce operator (like Amazon, Flipkart, etc.) who is required to collect tax at source
- Person engaged in inter-state supply of goods (however, there is no restriction on purchasing goods from inter-state suppliers)
- Person engaged in exports of goods (Exports are considered inter-state supply under GST law)
- A casual taxable person, i.e. a person who occasionally undertakes supplies in a state where he/she has no fixed place of business
- A non-resident taxable person, i.e., a person who occasionally undertakes supplies but has no fixed place of business or residence in India
- Person who has purchased any goods from unregistered dealer, unless he/she has paid GST on such goods on reverse charge basis
- Manufacturer of following goods:
    1. Ice cream and other edible ice
    2. Pan masala
    3. Tobacco and manufactured tobacco substitutes

Okay, is there anything else that I need to keep in mind?

A few conditions and restrictions do need to be followed. These are:

1. *Composition Scheme Should Be Availed for All Premises*: A person with a single PAN, who is registered in more than one state under GST, has to opt for composition scheme for all the premises in each state. He/she cannot opt for composition scheme in one state, while choosing regular scheme of tax payment in others. In fact, even if he/she were to opt for the regular scheme of paying tax in one state, all of his/her other registered premises in other states would become ineligible for composition scheme.
2. *Bill of Supply:* A person opting for composition scheme is not eligible to issue a tax invoice. He/she has to issue a bill of supply for every sale he/she makes and mention the words 'composition taxable person, not eligible to collect tax on supplies' at the top of every bill issued by him/her. The contents of a bill of supply are very similar to a regular tax invoice, except that, the former shows no

tax amount charged on the goods, whereas, a regular invoice should show tax amounts separately. In other words, a person opting to pay tax under composition scheme cannot charge tax separately in his/her sales invoice.

3. *Non-availability of Input Tax Credit:* Credit of taxes paid on purchases is not available as set-off against the liability to pay GST on sale of goods.
4. *Customer Not Eligible to Take Credit of Composition Tax:* A customer who purchases goods from a person registered under composition scheme is not eligible to take input tax credit, as he/she does not have a tax invoice on the basis of which input tax credit can be claimed.
5. *Validity of Composition Scheme:* The benefit of composition scheme can be availed till the aggregate turnover reaches the threshold limit in the current financial year. The option lapses on the day on which the aggregate turnover exceeds the threshold limit, anytime during the financial year.
6. *Other Requirements:* Mention the words 'composition taxable person' on every notice board or signboard, which should be displayed in a prominent place at every place of business.

What steps should I take now, if I want to opt for composition scheme?

You should first register yourself under GST. In case you already are, file an intimation with the GST authorities, declaring your intention to opt for composition scheme.

FIGURE 10.2

#DIY_tip

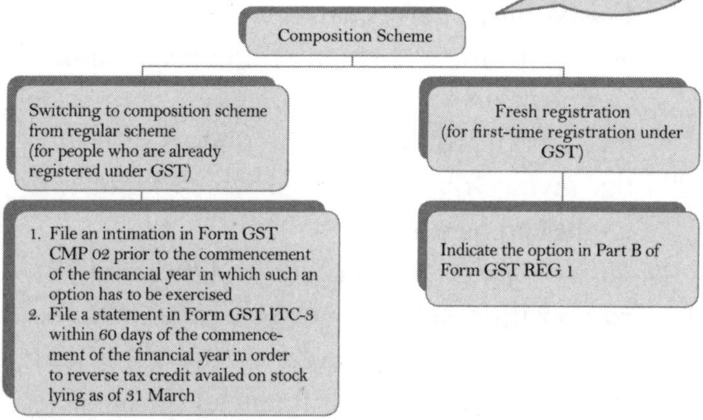

Note: Fresh declaration to opt for composition scheme is not required every year. A person can continue to pay tax under composition scheme, till he wishes to opt out of it.

FIGURE 10.3

Steps for filing intimation in Form GST CMP 02

Steps for detailed filing of GST REG 1 (Refer to Chapter 5)

Step 1: Login to www.gst.gov.in

Step 2: Go to 'Services' >'Registration' > 'Application to Opt for Composition Levy' *(as shown in Figure 10.4).*

FIGURE 10.4

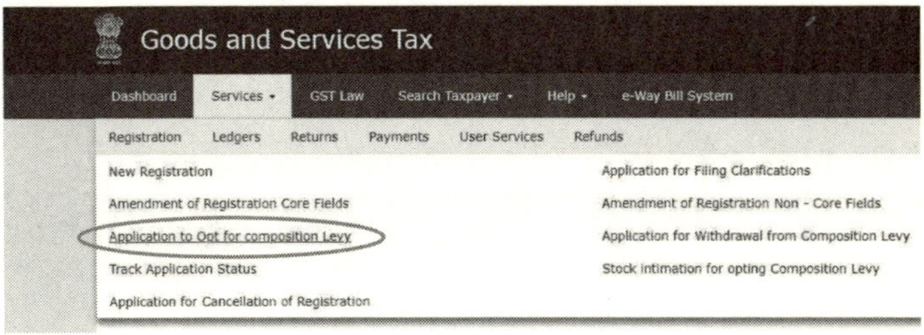

Step 3: Fill up the form and at the bottom, check the boxes 'Composition Declaration' and 'Verification'. Select the 'Name of Authorized Signatory' and enter 'Place'.

'Designation' and 'Date' would be auto populated. Click on 'Save'.

FIGURE 10.5

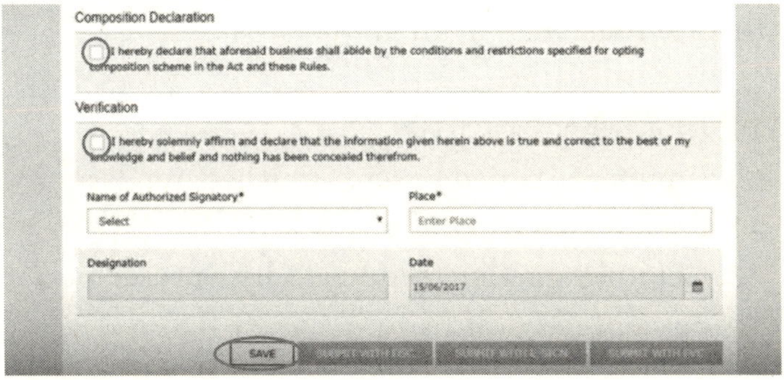

Step 4: Submit the form using either of the options mentioned.

Step 5: Once the form is submitted, a 'Success' message will be displayed.

An acknowledgment on the registered mobile number and email id is also sent.

FIGURE 10.6

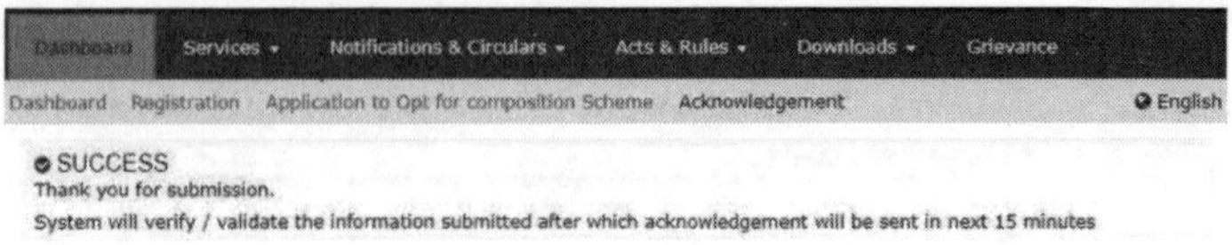

Once the intimation in Form GST CMP-02 has been filed, a statement under Form GST ITC-3 has to be filed within 60 days of the commencement of the financial year for which composition scheme has been opted for. GST ITC-3 has to be filed for reversal of input tax credit on goods, outstanding as on 31 March of the previous year, availed on:

1. Inputs held as stock.
2. Inputs contained in semi-finished goods and finished goods held in stock.
3. Capital goods, reduced by prescribed percentage points.

Since input tax credit is not allowed under the composition scheme, it is essential that this be filed; otherwise, tax authorities may deny applicability of the scheme.

It is to be noted that this statement has to be filed only by a person switching from regular scheme to composition scheme. If a person is registering afresh under GST, he/she need not file GST ITC-3 as he/she will not have stock with him/her on which he/she has already availed input tax credit.

#DIY_tip

Steps to file GST ITC-3 are as follows:
Step 1: Login to www.gst.gov.in.
Step 2: Go to 'Services' >'Returns> 'ITC Forms'.

FIGURE 10.7

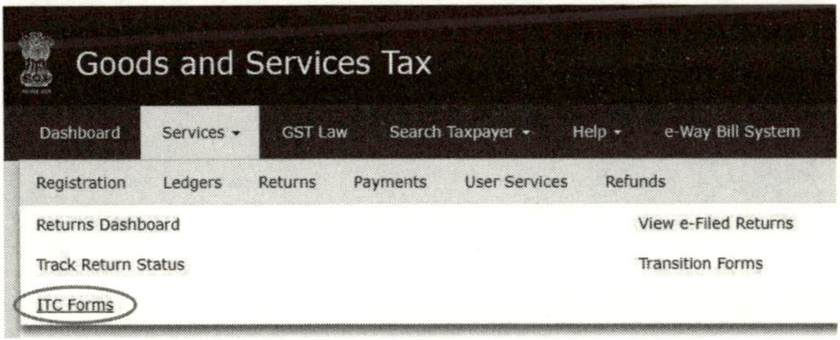

Step 3: Under GST ITC-03 capsule, either of the two options can be selected, viz.: 'Prepare Online' or 'Prepare Offline'.

1. *Offline Mode:* Download the offline utility from homepage ('www.gst.gov.in' > 'Downloads' > 'Offline Tools' > 'FORM GST ITC-03 Offline Tool')

   Fill data in the excel sheet as per given instructions > login to GST portal > upload file after clicking 'Prepare Offline'.
2. *Online Mode*: Select 'Prepare Online'. The steps for online filing of data can be seen in Figure 10.8

FIGURE 10.8

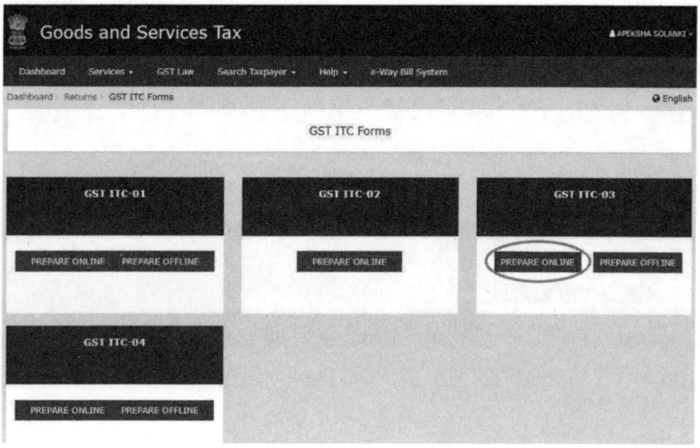

Step 4: Select option 4(a), i.e. option applicable for taxpayers opting for composition scheme.

Step 5: Once said option has been selected, the screen shown in Figure 10.9 is displayed.

Each tab should now be filled individually, with the relevant data.

FIGURE 10.9

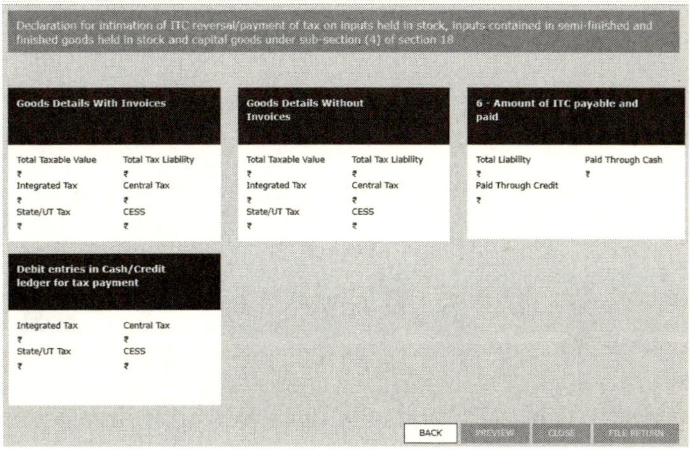

The following steps would describe in detail the manner in which each tab should be filled.

Step 6: Tab1:'Goods Details With Invoices'.

Fill in all the particulars of an invoice and click 'Add'. The next invoice details should be filled in, in the same manner.

After all invoices have been added, click the 'Save' button.

Note: 'Date from which exemption is effective' is the date on which composition scheme has been opted for.

FIGURE 10.10

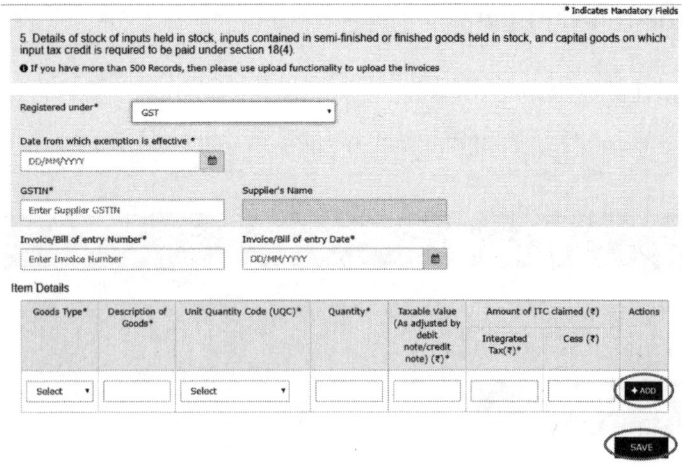

Step 7: Tab 2: 'Goods Details Without Invoices'. Tab 2 has exactly the same details as Tab 1, except for 'Invoice/Bill of Entry Number' and 'Invoice/Bill of Entry Date'.

Once Tab 2 has been saved, a screen asking for details of a chartered accountant or cost accountant would pop up. Details of a CA are required because invoices are missing and, therefore, the value of the goods would be based on the market value of similar goods, which will have to be certified by a CA.

The certificate of a CA valuing the goods has to be uploaded.

Click 'Save CA Details'.

FIGURE 10.11

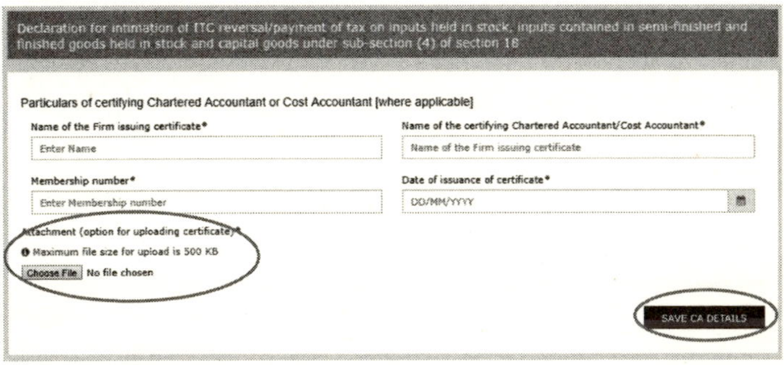

Step 8: Tab 3: 'Amount of ITC Payable and Paid' tab.

The cash and credit balance available in the ledger is shown in the first tab.

The credit which has to be reversed can be paid through cash ledger. If there is no cash available in the ledger, then cash payment can be made by generating a challan (challan can be paid either through online payment gateway or over the counter).

Click on 'Make Payment'.

FIGURE 10.12

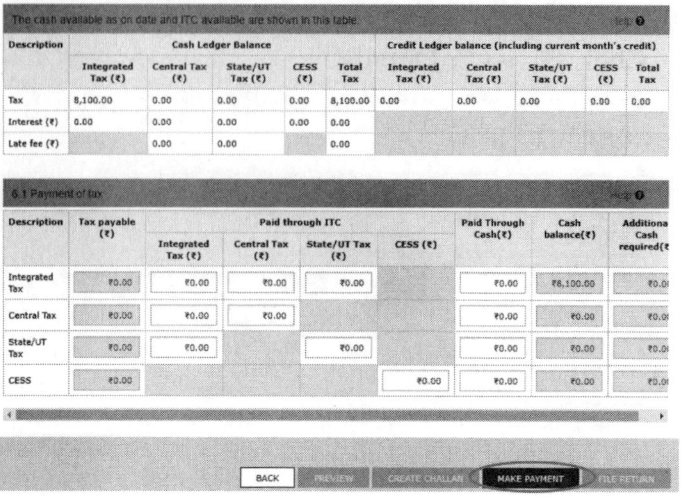

The cash available as on date and ITC available are shown in this table. Help

Description	Cash Ledger Balance					Credit Ledger balance (including current month's credit)				
	Integrated Tax (₹)	Central Tax (₹)	State/UT Tax (₹)	CESS (₹)	Total Tax	Integrated Tax (₹)	Central Tax (₹)	State/UT Tax (₹)	CESS (₹)	Total Tax
Tax	8,100.00	0.00	0.00	0.00	8,100.00	0.00	0.00	0.00	0.00	0.00
Interest (₹)	0.00	0.00	0.00	0.00	0.00					
Late fee (₹)		0.00	0.00		0.00					

6.1 Payment of tax Help

Description	Tax payable (₹)	Paid through ITC				Paid Through Cash(₹)	Cash balance(₹)	Additiona Cash required(₹
		Integrated Tax (₹)	Central Tax (₹)	State/UT Tax (₹)	CESS (₹)			
Integrated Tax	₹0.00	₹0.00	₹0.00	₹0.00		₹0.00	₹8,100.00	₹0.0
Central Tax	₹0.00	₹0.00	₹0.00			₹0.00	₹0.00	₹0.0
State/UT Tax	₹0.00	₹0.00		₹0.00		₹0.00	₹0.00	₹0.0
CESS	₹0.00				₹0.00	₹0.00	₹0.00	₹0.0

BACK PREVIEW CREATE CHALLAN MAKE PAYMENT FILE RETURN

Step 9: Once payment is made, click 'Ok'.

FIGURE 10.13

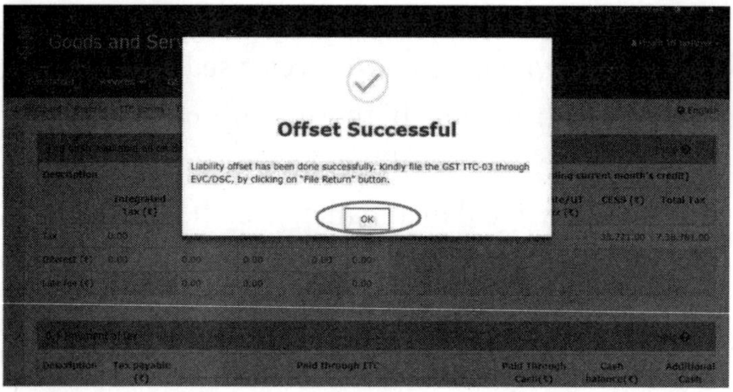

Step 10: Tab 4: 'Debit Entries in Cash/Credit Ledger for Tax Payment'

This tab is autopopulated and can be viewed to see the final outcome of reversal of ITC.

Step 11: Click 'File Return' > 'Preview Draft ITC-03' > Check the Box for 'Declaration' and select 'Authorised Signatory' > 'File With DSC/ EVC' > 'Proceed'.

Is it possible that our option to file tax under composition scheme be denied or cancelled?

Yes, option to pay tax under composition scheme can be denied. In such a case, you can undertake the steps illustrated in Figure 10.14.

FIGURE 10.14

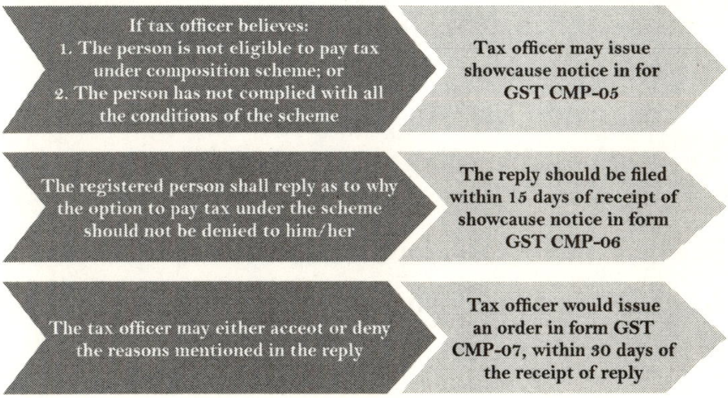

And is it possible to shift from composition scheme to regular scheme of paying taxes?

Yes, that can be done in the following situations:

1. A person may withdraw from the scheme if he is unable to comply with the conditions of the composition scheme. For example, if his/her turnover crosses the threshold limit during the financial year, then, within seven days, he/she should file an intimation to withdraw from the scheme.
2. A person may withdraw if he/she does not wish to pay taxes under the composition scheme and finds it beneficial to pay tax under regular scheme.
3. He/she may also be compelled to shift from one scheme to the other if the tax officer has issued an order under GST CMP-07, denying the option to pay tax under composition scheme.

In all of these cases, the person is required to file an intimation in Form GST CMP-04 in order to withdraw from the composition scheme.

Note: Withdrawal from composition scheme from a place of business in one state would mean withdrawal from all places of business in other states also registered under the same PAN.

Once a person has withdrawn from composition scheme and has started paying taxes under regular scheme, he has to do the following:

1. Issue tax invoice instead of bill of supply.
2. He would be eligible to claim input tax credit on the goods lying in stock and also on capital goods. For this, intimation in Form GST ITC-01, has to be filed within 30 days from the date from which the option to pay tax under composition scheme has been withdrawn.

Can you just help me with one last thing? How does one pay taxes and file returns under composition scheme?

A person opting for composition scheme has to file only one annual return in Form GSTR-4 and the tax has to be paid quarterly in Form GST CMP-08. Form GST CMP-08 is a statement cum challan, where self-assessed tax is paid by composition taxpayers. This is beneficial for small business persons as it would save a lot of compliance cost and efforts.

TABLE 10.2

Particulars	Due Date	Form
Quarterly Tax Payments	18th of the month succeeding the quarter	
April–June	18 July	CMP-08
July–September	18 October	CMP-08
October–December	18 January	CMP-08
January–March	18 April	CMP-08
Annual Return	30 April (30 April of the next financial year)	GSTR 4/ GSTR 9A

Note: Due dates of return for any period may be extended by the tax authorities

The steps to file a return under composition scheme in Form GSTR-4 are very similar to the steps taken to file a regular return in Form GSTR-1 *(as discussed in Chapter 5)*. Form GST CMP-08 can also be filed on similar lines.

Thank you, GG, for all your help. Composition scheme does seem easy and something that I can probably manage on my own. I'm sure a lot of people must have opted for one?

As of July 2019, around 17% of the total number of people registered under GST have registered for composition levy. A lot of small business persons whose turnover is below ₹1.5 crore have still opted for regular scheme instead of composition scheme.

Why is that?

Composition schemes have a few cons, one of which is that, it does not really make the scheme very cost-effective for small business persons. Some of them end up paying *more* taxes under composition scheme than they would under regular scheme.

But will they not incur more compliance costs under regular scheme? A higher number of returns would have to be filed, detailed accounts and records would have to be maintained, all of which would only augment the fee of a chartered accountant. Also, the time and effort that a taxpayer would have to invest into filing returns under regular scheme is much more. Why then, would they choose the latter over composition scheme?

The cost of compliance, along with taxes paid, under regular scheme is actually less than the amount of tax small business persons may shell out under composition scheme, in some cases. Small traders have very little margin, and tax at 1% of turnover is much more than the overall tax that they would actually pay under regular scheme (where set-off of tax credit is also available).

Some of the major disadvantages of composition scheme are:

1. *Tax is Charged Even on Exempt Sales:* The biggest disadvantage under composition scheme is that concessional rate of tax is also levied on exempt sales. Such sales are not taxable under regular scheme, but under composition scheme, they attract GST, which adds to the cost of the taxpayer.
2. *Tax Invoice Cannot Be Issued:* A lot of regular scheme purchasers do not want to deal with composition scheme sellers because that blocks their input credit chain, as tax invoice cannot be issued by a dealer under composition scheme. This forces small vendors also to join the regular scheme of paying taxes, lest they lose customers.

3. *Input Tax Credit Not Available:* Composition dealers are not allowed to avail input tax credit, which is a big disadvantage to these small dealers. Since in a lot of cases, the margins of trading are not very high, 1% of tax on turnover under composition scheme adds to a substantial amount of cost when input tax credit is not available. This also forces a lot of small business persons to opt for regular scheme.
4. *No Inter-state Sales Are Allowed:* Interstate sales are not allowed under composition scheme. This automatically eliminates a lot of small business persons dealing in inter-state sales.
5. *Exports Are Not Allowed:* Exports are considered inter-state sales under GST and, hence, small dealers engaged in exports are also eliminated from the scheme.
6. *Sale Through E-commerce Portal is Not Allowed:* A person, under composition scheme, cannot sell through an e-commerce portal. This is a very big deterrent in times when use of technology is increasing at such a fast pace.
7. *Purchases from Unregistered Dealer:* Purchases from unregistered dealers attract tax under reverse charge mechanism,

which again increases compliance for small business persons.

#GG_tip

Thus, we can conclude that a small business person should probably undertake due diligence of his/her business and analyse which method of payment of taxes would benefit him/her the most, instead of blindly going in for composition scheme.

How GST Affects a Household

GST on Products Sold at MRP

I just hate this whole GST thing. Everything has become so expensive! I'm sure my monthly household shopping bills must have increased by approximately 20%!

Why do you say so?

I was just at the super market, and on top of my total bill of ₹2,000, I had to pay an extra amount of GST at 18%! I never paid any taxes on grocery bills earlier. How is Modi ji's *acche din* happening?

You paid GST on a grocery bill?

Yes! Did I have a choice?

Don't you know that you're not supposed to pay GST on products with an MRP? MRP is the Maximum Retail Price and, as its name implies, it is the maximum price that can be charged for a product. It is calculated by the manufacturer and printed on the product, so a retailer cannot charge more than the MRP from a buyer. It is the final price and includes everything, even taxes. The MRP printed on the product includes GST.

Really? He told me that, after introduction of GST, prices of the products have risen and, hence, GST has to be charged separately, over and above the MRP of the products.

It is not that GST has only increased the prices of the product. GST has been beneficial to a lot of industries, where prices of products have even decreased because of it. But MRP can be changed or altered only by the manufacturer and not by the retailers.

So have manufacturers altered the MRPs of products after the introduction of GST?

Yes, a lot of manufacturers *have* altered (either through increase or decrease of) the

MRP, post introduction of GST. The government has instructed manufacturers to advertise (with at least two advertisements) any revision of MRP of unsold, pre-packaged products in at least two newspapers. The revised MRP should be displayed through stickers on the product, online printing or stamping and the old MRP should also be visible next to the new revised MRP.

Okay, I get it. So we are not supposed to pay GST on products with MRP, because MRP includes taxes too, right?

Absolutely correct!

Okay, but the other day, my friends and I had gone shopping. There was a flat 40% discount on clothes. After giving us a discount on the MRP of the product, however, the shopkeeper charged GST on the dicounted value of that product. The store manager said that if we bought the product at full MRP value, then we would not be charged any GST, but since we were buying at a discounted value, GST would be charged. Although his logic seemed absurd, we had no choice, because he was standing his ground and

would not sell the product without charging GST on the discounted price.

That logic is nonsense. He is simply charging extra money in the name of GST and enriching himself. If he is giving you a 40% discount on the MRP, then he cannot charge GST over and above that. MRP *includes* GST and so, the consumer is already paying tax on the purchase. The discounted price would also include the element of GST and does not need to be loaded with any additional tax. He is essentially giving you less than the supposed 40% discount on the product by levying an additional charge in the guise of GST.

Is there a way I can get back at that store manager and the grocery shop owner?

Yes, absolutely! To register a complaint against such shopkeepers, you can use the following methods:

1. Call the National Consumer Helpline number: 1800 11 4000 or 14404.
2. File a complaint through the 'UMANG' app which can be downloaded through Google or Apple playstore (once the app

has been downloaded and initial set-up has been completed, type 'national consumer helpline' in the search bar and then register the complaint).

3. You can even file a complaint online.

#DIY_tip

The following steps will help you file an online complaint:

Step 1: 'Sign up' at https://consumerhelpline.gov.in/.

FIGURE 11.1

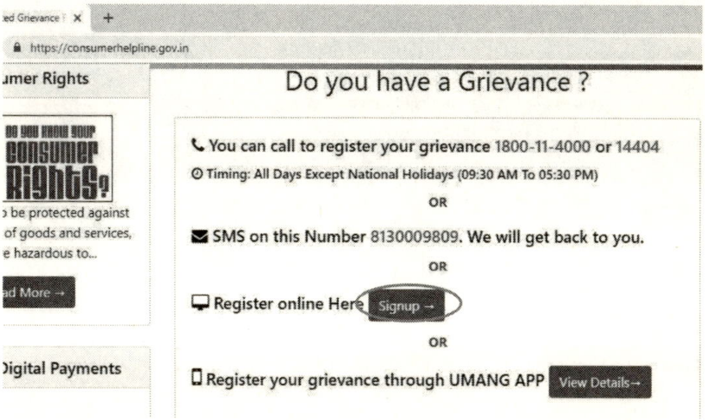

Step 2: Fill the 'Consumer Registration Form' and click on 'Sign Up'.

FIGURE 11.2

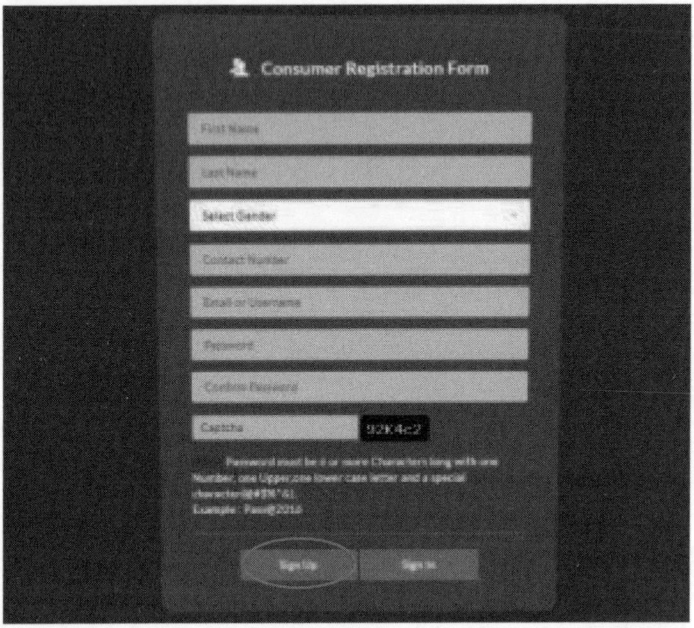

Step 3: The following message will be displayed on the screen: 'Well done: Registration successful, please verify in the registered email id'.

Login to the email id that you used in the consumer registration form earlier and verify, as per the instructions given in the email.

Once consumer verification is complete, click 'Sign In' to sign into your consumer account.

FIGURE 11.3

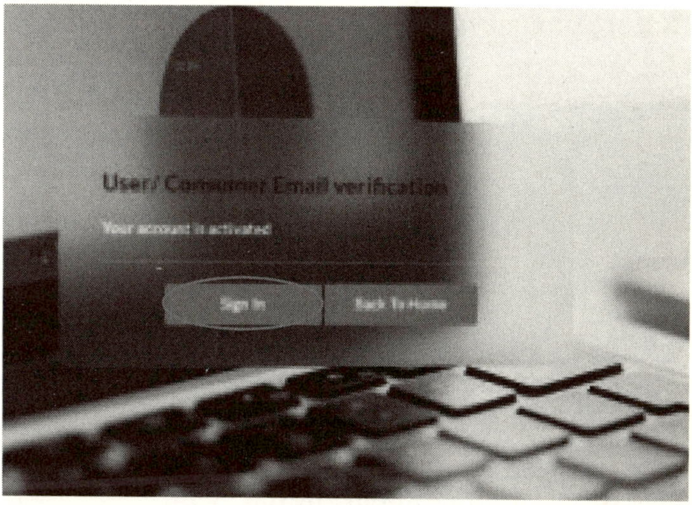

Click 'I Agree' to open the 'Grievance Registration Form'.

Step 4: From the dropdown menu, select 'Grievance', to file a complaint against the shopkeeper.

FIGURE 11.4

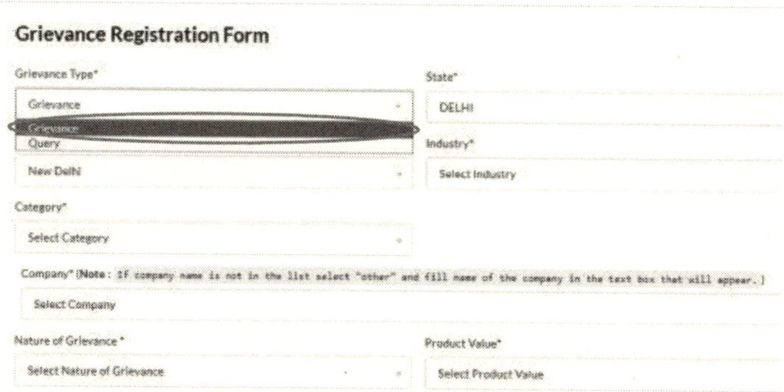

Step 5: Select the appropriate option under the 'Nature of Grievance' tab.

FIGURE 11.5

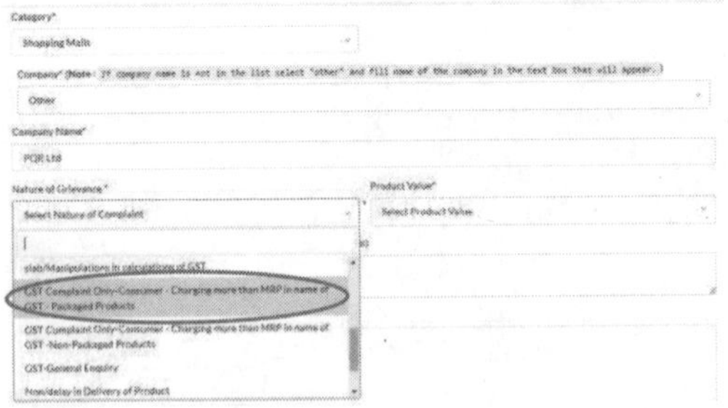

Step 6: Fill in other details in the form.
Describe the complaint.
Upload proof, such as the invoice where GST has been charged on the MRP.
Click 'Submit'.
Note: A complaint will not be considered valid, unless valid proof is available with the consumer.

FIGURE 11.6

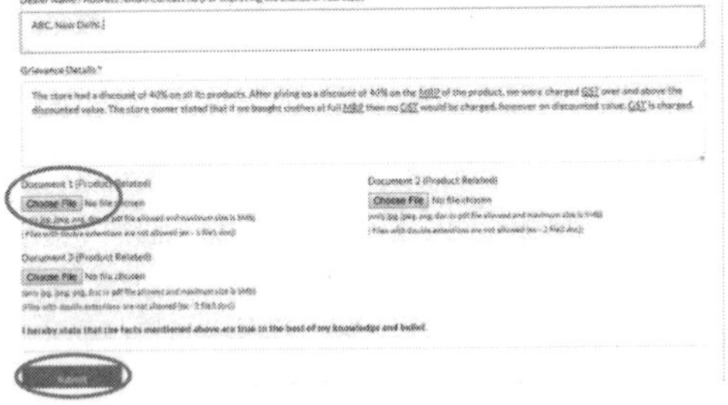

Step 7: After successful submission of the form, the status of the grievance can be tracked by clicking the tab on the left side of the screen.

FIGURE 11.7

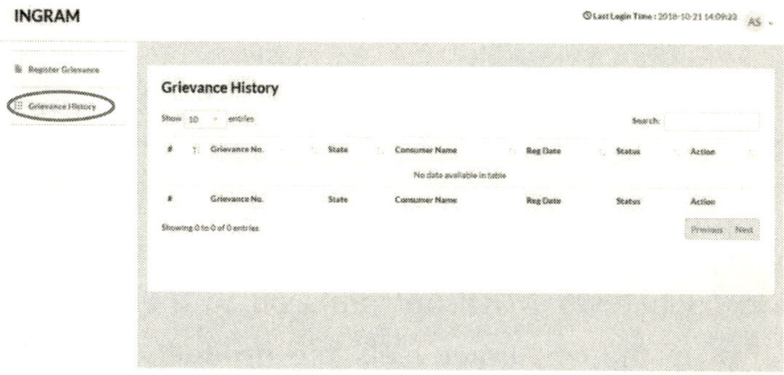

Thanks for the help. Also, the other day when I went out to dine at a restaurant, they charged me ₹50 for 1 litre bottle of packaged water. At the local shops, we only pay ₹20 for the same product! The restaurant totally overcharged us. I guess I should file a complaint against them too.

You were not cheated that day. Some restaurants, movie halls, hotels or airlines get special MRPs printed on water bottles, packets of chips or other items, so that they can charge a higher amount. As per Indian laws, a retailer cannot sell the products at more than the MRP. However, if the MRP printed on the product is higher than the usual MRP at other outlets, then the retailer can charge such a higher amount, upto the MRP printed on the product.

Is this legal? 

 Absolutely! A manufacturer can print whatever MRP he wants on to the product. If the consumer feels the product is highly priced, then they are at liberty to not buy it.

 Okay. GG there is one more thing. I am getting married soon and I have to start preparing for it. My wife and I will set up our house from scratch and we are worried that, with the introduction of GST, our expenses may shoot up!

 What are the things that you need to buy? Maybe I can help you budget for everything accordingly.

 Firstly, I wanted to buy an engagement ring for my wife. I was wondering if jewellery

rates have gone up because of GST. Apart from that, the major expenses would be the household basics: furniture, household appliances, electronic items, food items and other daily-use articles. Would our budget increase, factoring in GST?

Well, let us see how GST would affect your expenses on most of these common-use items, category wise.

GST on Jewellery

GST rates on gold jewellery have increased marginally as compared to the pre-GST regime. Gold jewellery is now taxed at the rate of 3% compared to approximate taxes amounting to 2.5% earlier (excise duty + VAT).

It is to be noted that when a customer goes to buy a gold article at a jeweller, tax at 3% will be charged on the total value of the gold article, whether or not making charges are shown separately. For example, if a customer goes to buy a gold chain worth ₹30,000 (the value of gold being ₹28,000 and making charges amounting to ₹2,000), then GST would be charged at 3% on the total transaction value of ₹30,000.

GST Impact on Basic Food Items

FIGURE 11.8

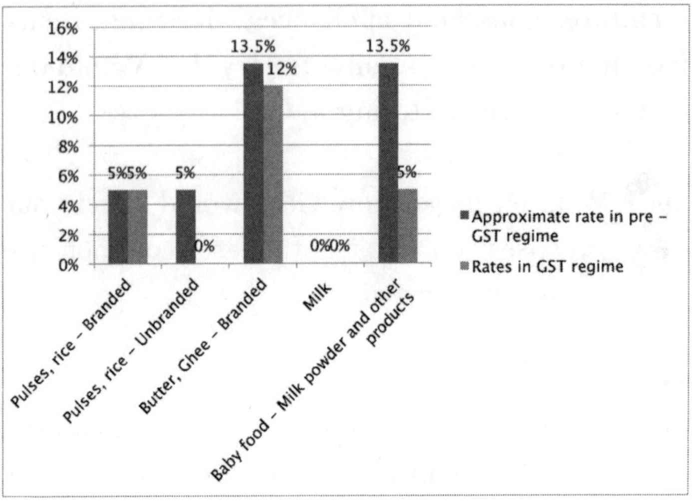

Note: Rates indicated above in pre and post-GST regime are approximate indicators of the broad category in which various products lie.

Pre-GST rates are a total of excise duty and an approximate average VAT rate (VAT rates vary state-wise).

GST Impact on White Goods and Other Household Items

FIGURE 11.9

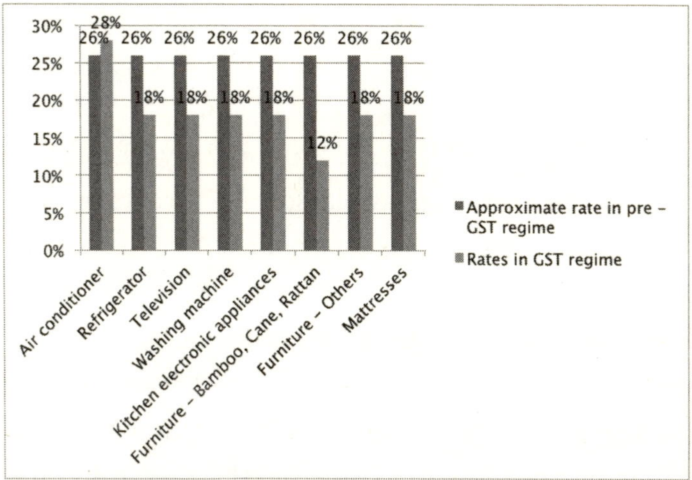

Note: Post and pre-GST rates are indicative.

Pre-GST rates are approximate indicators of total of excise duty and VAT rate (VAT rates vary state-wise).

GST Impact on Personal Care Products, Clothes, Etc.

FIGURE 11.10

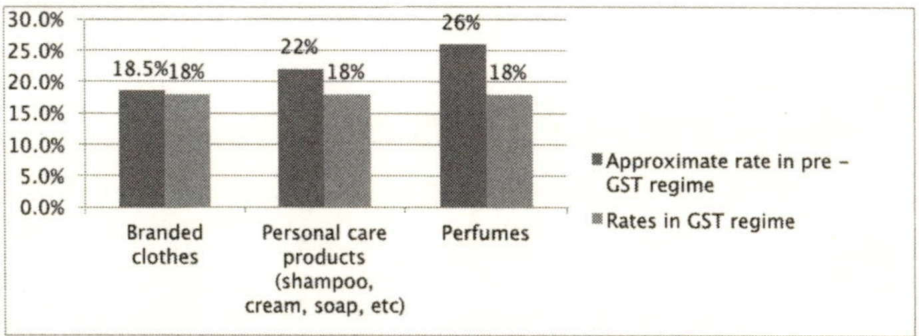

Note: Rates indicated above in pre- and post-GST regime are approximate indicators of the broad category in which various products lie.

Pre-GST rates are a total of excise duty and an approximate average VAT rate (VAT rates vary state-wise).

Figures 11.8, 11.9 and 11.10 clearly indicate that GST rates have reduced on most products. Also, since GST is the only tax levied at each stage in the consumer chain (i.e. from manufacturer to end consumer), credit set-off is available at every stage. This also reduces the cost of the product and ultimately, the MRP of the product may be reduced. Earlier, credit was not available for central taxes (like excise duty and service tax) against VAT liability to be paid, and hence, taxes formed part of the cost of the product. Since central taxes formed part of the cost of the product, VAT would be levied on price inclusive of central taxes, which lead to a situation of tax on tax. This also increased the tax burden and eventually, the price of the product increased. It can, therefore, be concluded that consumers would benefit to a large extent from GST on these products.

Okay, I am glad to know that GST will not affect our budget a lot. What about the prices that we would have to incur on our honeymoon? Hotel stay, air fares/rail fares and cab expenses—would they also be impacted by GST?

We can see the impact of GST on these in the Table 11.1:

GST Impact on Hotels, Air/Rail Travel, Radio Taxis

TABLE 11.1

Category	Taxability under Pre-GST Regime (Service Tax and/ or VAT)*	Taxability under GST Regime*	Impact on Cost of Services Post GST Regime**	Conditions under Pre and Post-GST Regime
Hotel Accommodation Where room rent per day is: Less than ₹1,000	Exempt	Exempt	↔	-
>=₹1,000 <₹2,500	15%–40%	12%	↓	
>=₹2,500 <₹7,500	15%–40%	18%	↓/↑	
> ₹7,500	15%–40%	28%	↓/↑	
Air Travel: Economy Class	6%	5%	↓	Subject to prescribed restrictions on set-off of full credit availability against the output liability to pay taxes
Other	9%	12%	↑	

»

Category	Taxability under Pre-GST Regime (Service Tax and/ or VAT)*	Taxability under GST Regime*	Impact on Cost of Services Post GST Regime**	Conditions under Pre and Post-GST Regime
Travel by Rail	4.5%	5%	↑	Subject to prescribed restrictions on set-off of full credit availability against the output liability to pay taxes
Radio Taxis (Like Ola/ Uber)	6%	5%	↓	Subject to prescribed restrictions on set-off of full credit availability against the output liability to pay taxes

**The tax rates are indicative.*

** Indicators: ⟷ *Same tax impact as pre-GST era;* ↓ *Decrease in tax burden post GST;* ↑ *Increase in tax burden post GST*

Phew! I think I'm a little stress-free now. The impact of GST on most products or services seems to be a positive one.

GST for a Student: Millennials Fretting Over Low Pocket Money?

Namaste GG. Needed your advice on a few things. In college, we were discussing whether we would have to demand for higher pocket money because of GST. Could you guide me a bit with my queries?

Of course, I would!

What happens to my education fee? Does GST make my education costly?

GST Impact on Educational Institutions

The government has always been very sensitive about education in our country.

The government has a constitutional obligation to provide free and compulsory elementary education to every child. Hence, it has always strived to keep basic education tax free.

Before we get into the details of the impact of GST on the education sector, let us first see what an educational institution means, as per the GST law.

An educational institution means an institution providing services by way of:

1. Pre-school education and education up to higher secondary school or equivalent;
2. Education as a part of a curriculum for obtaining a qualification recognised by any law in India; or
3. Education as a part of an approved vocational education course.

GST impact on different educational institutions can be seen in the following ways:

1. *Educational Institution Providing Pre-school and Education up to Higher Secondary School (PS-HSS:)*
   (a) Any services provided by PS-HSS to its students, faculty or staff do not attract GST.

(b) PS-HSS does not have to pay GST for availing following services from a third-party vendor:
   (i) Transportation of students, faculty or other staff.
   (ii) Catering services.
   (iii) Security, cleaning or housekeeping services.
   (iv) Services relating to admission to or conduct of examination, by such institution.

This makes it clear that any services provided by or availed by PS-HSS would not attract GST. The same taxability was prevalent even in the pre-GST era. Hence, there would be no change in the school fee of a student.

However, it is important to note that any other services availed by PS-HSS from a private player apart from the four services listed above (like canteen, repairs and maintenance service, etc.) would attract GST at the rate of 18%. In the pre-GST era, the same was taxable at the rate of 15%. PS-HSS would have to shell out more money to avail such services by 3% after introduction of GST.

2. *Higher Educational Institution (HEI): Colleges/ Universities:* Services provided by HEI (which provides a qualification recognised by a law in India) do not attract GST. This means that a student enrolling in HEI does not have to pay GST on the fee paid to HEI. However, while the students would not directly pay GST to HEI, they would still have to bear the cost of GST indirectly.

   HEIs have to pay GST on most of the services availed by them. These services availed by them would be charged at the rate of 18% (this being higher by 3% compared to erstwhile service tax rate). Since there is no tax on services provided by HEI, credit of taxes paid on services availed will not be available as a set-off to HEI. This would increase the cost of procurement for HEI which, in turn, may be reflected in the fee of the student. Students would, therefore, have to bear the brunt of higher rate of taxes.
3. *Hostel Facilities Provided by Schools, Colleges or Universities:* Any service provided by an educational institution to its students, faculty or staff, will not attract GST, which means hostel facilities provided by any educational institution will be tax free. Students do not have to bear GST on hostel fees charged by educational institutions.

4. *Boarding Schools:* Boarding schools provide educational services along with other services like residence and food to students. This category of services comes under composite/bundled supply of service.

Composite/bundled supply of services mean when a service supplied by one person to another comprises of two or more supply of services or goods. Such services are naturally bundled and are provided together in the natural course of business. Such services are generally sold as a combination. For example, in case of Movers and Packers, they provide service of packing of goods, transportation of goods, insuring the goods and loading and unloading the goods. All these services are naturally bundled together and a lump sum fee for transportation of goods is charged by Movers and Packers.

Service provided by boarding schools is also a bundled supply as a lump sum fee is charged, for providing education, boarding and food services to students. In such cases, taxability of the principal/main supply (which is providing education in the current scenario) will determine the taxability of the entire bundled service. Since education is tax free under GST, fee charged by boarding schools from students does not include GST.

5. *Government Schools:* Any activity or transaction undertaken by the Central government, any state government or any local authority shall not be treated as supply of goods or services. Therefore, there will be no tax on education provided by government or municipal schools.
6. *Indian Institute of Management (IIM):* The following courses provided by IIM do not attract GST:
   (a) Two-year full-time Post-Graduate Programme in Management (PGP), admissions to which are made on the basis of Common Admission Test (CAT).
   (b) Fellow Programme in Management (FPM).
   (c) Five-Year Integrated Programme in Management (IPM).

However, the Executive Development Programme under an IIM is subject to GST.

7. *National Skill Development Corporation (NSDC):* The definition of an educational institution also covers any institution

providing education as a part of an approved vocational education course. Accordingly, any fee paid to NSDC for an approved vocational course does not attract GST.

8. *Charitable Trusts:* Income from education is wholly exempt from GST if a charitable trust is running a school, college or educational institution for abandoned persons, orphans, homeless children, physically or mentally abused persons, prisoners or persons over the age of 65 years or above residing in a rural area.

All of the above can be summarised as follows in Table 12.1:

TABLE 12.1

Category	Taxability under Service Tax Regime	Taxability under GST Regime	Impact on Cost of Services Post Introduction of GST *
Pre-school and Education up to Higher Secondary School (PS-HSS):			
• Service provided by PS-HSS to students, faculty or staff	Exempt	Exempt	↔
• All major services provided to PS-HSS by third party vendors	Exempt	Exempt	↔

»

»

Category	Taxability under Service Tax Regime	Taxability under GST Regime	Impact on Cost of Services Post Introduction of GST *
HEI - Colleges/ Universities: • Service provided by HEI to students, faculty or staff • Services provided to HEI by third party vendors	Exempt 15%	Exempt 18%	↔ ↑ *(The fee of a student may increase due to increase in the cost of procurement of services by HEI)*
Hostel Facilities Provided by Schools, Colleges or Universities	Exempt	Exempt	↔
Boarding Schools	Exempt	Exempt	↔
Government Schools	Exempt	Exempt	↔
Indian Institute of Management (IIM): 1. Two-year full-time Post-Graduate Programmes in Management 2. Fellow Programme in Management; and 3. Five-Year Integrated Programme in Management 4. Executive Development Programme	Exempt Exempt Exempt 15%	Exempt Exempt Exempt 18%	↔ ↔ ↔ ↑

*Indicators: ↔ *Same tax impact as pre-GST era;* ↑ *Increase in tax burden post GST*

Thank you, GG, for the detailed gyan on impact of GST on various types of educational institutions. But how about the other expenses that may affect students like me living away from my parents and hometown? Would my expenses on paying guests, laundry, coaching classes, etc. increase because of GST?

Sure, let me discuss the impact of GST on each of these.

TABLE 12.2

Category	Taxability under Service Tax Regime	Taxability under GST Regime	Impact on Cost of Services Post GST Regime*
Coaching Institutes	15%	18% *(coaching institutes do not fall in the definition of educational institution as defined by GST law)*	↑
Paying Guest *(where room rent per day is less than ₹1,000)*	Exempt	Exempt	↔
Laundry Services (dry or wet cleaning of clothes)	15%	18%	↑

Category	Taxability under Service Tax Regime	Taxability under GST Regime	Impact on Cost of Services Post GST Regime*
Telecom Services: Mobile phone connection (like Vodafone, Airtel, etc.)	15%	18%	↑
Broadband Connection	15%	18%	↑

** **Indicators:** ⟷ Same tax impact as pre-GST era; ↑ Increase in tax burden post GST*

Well, it seems like GST is going to burn a hole in my pocket for a lot of things! How about the impact on other entertainment stuff, which students like me often like to do? Like, going to movies or eating at restaurants?

GST Impact on Restaurant Bills

Well, you guys can rejoice as far as restaurant bills are concerned. The impact of GST on restaurant bills is a positive one. You could see this under Table 12.3.

TABLE 12.3

Category of Restaurant	GST Rates	Conditions
All Restaurants (with or without air conditioning)	5%	GST paid on purchase of goods and services by restaurants is not available for set-off against GST to be deposited with the government
Restaurants within Hotels (where room tariff is less than ₹7,500)	5%	GST paid on purchase of goods and services by restaurants is not available for set-off against GST to be deposited with the government
Restaurants within Hotels (where room tariff is more than ₹7,500)	18%	GST paid on purchase of goods and services by restaurants is available for set-off against GST to be deposited with the government

In comparison to Table 12.3, the taxes in the pre-GST regime can be seen under Table 12.4.

TABLE 12.4

Pre-GST taxes	Rate of tax
Service Tax	6% *(No set-off of taxes paid on services availed by restaurants was available against the service tax to be deposited with the government)*
VAT	14.5% *(VAT rates varied according to each state)*
Total	20.5%

We can better understand the impact of GST on restaurants with an example, as that seen in Table 12.5

TABLE 12.5

(All numbers in INR)

Particulars	Taxability under Service Tax Regime	Taxability under GST Regime
Total Value of Bill [A]	1,000	1,000
Total Input Tax Credit Available [B] (VAT/GST)	100	100
Tax on Total Value of Bill: [C] Service Tax @ 6% VAT @ 14.5% GST @ 5%	 60 145 -	 - - 50
Output Tax Liability (to be deposited with the government by restaurants): [C-B] ST (no input tax credit available) VAT (145-100) GST(no input tax credit available)	 60 45 	 50
TOTAL VALUE OF BILL *(including taxes)*[A+C] *(to be paid by the customers)*	1,205	1,050

It is obvious that tax liability to be borne by the restaurant owners under GST regime is only ₹50 as compared to ₹105 (60+45) under the pre-GST era. Although input tax credit is not available (in most cases of restaurant type) under GST, in the pre-GST era, input tax credit was available only for VAT (under service tax, abatement was provided, and hence, no credit of input tax was available). The overall impact of burden of taxes, taking into consideration availability of input tax credit and rate of taxes, has drastically reduced under GST regime.

Okay, but I have still seen a lot of restaurants charge both VAT and GST in their bill. Isn't that wrong?

The restaurants charge VAT only on alcohol. Since alcohol for human consumption is outside the purview of GST, the old regime of VAT is still applicable on it. On other food items, GST is applicable. Hence, a restaurant bill will have both VAT and GST applicable, with VAT only on the price of alcohol and GST on the remaining bill.

But what about service charge that was charged earlier and continues to be charged even under GST?

Service charge is not a tax. It is not charged or collected by the government. It is a charge collected by the restaurants in place of the 'tips' that people mostly pay to the attendant at the restaurants. Generally, the amount paid under service charge gets distributed to waiters, kitchen staff and cleaning staff by the restaurant owners. Hence, if a bill has service charge levied on it, then the customers may not pay 'tip' separately to the waiters. GST has no impact on service charge and this is irrespective of the tax laws in the country.

Okay, and what about the impact of GST on movie tickets?

GST Impact on Movie Tickets

The impact of GST on movies can be seen in Table 12.6.

TABLE 12.6

Particulars	Taxability under GST Regime	Taxability under Pre-GST Regime
Taxes Levied	GST at the rate of 18% is applicable on the sale of movie tickets above ₹100 and at the rate of 12% on sale of movie tickets up to ₹100	No service tax or VAT was applicable on sale of movie tickets

Particulars	Taxability under GST Regime	Taxability under Pre-GST Regime
State or Local Entertainment Taxes	In a few states, local entertainment taxes on sale of movie tickets is applicable (over and above GST)	State entertainment tax on sale of movie tickets was applicable (the rate of tax ranged from 0% to 110% in different states)
Food and Beverage in Movie Halls	GST at the rate of 18% on the sale of food and beverage is applicable. However, if it is treated as cafeteria/ restaurant, 5% of GST may be payable without the benefit of input tax credit	Service tax: 6% VAT: 14.5% (varies according to each state) Total tax burden (on an average): 20.5%
Input Tax Credit	Credit of GST paid on renting of premise, catering, etc. can be set off against GST liability on sale of movie tickets	State entertainment tax was levied on sale of movie tickets. Therefore, service tax or VAT paid by movie halls on renting of premises, catering services, security services, etc. was not available as set-off against entertainment tax. These taxes formed part of the cost to the movie theatre and became part of price of the ticket. Entertainment tax was levied on the entire amount of the price of the ticket, which led to a situation of tax on tax

Table 12.6 shows that the impact of GST on sale of movie tickets may vary in each state. Where entertainment tax was as high at 110%, GST would be a big relief in such states. However, in states where entertainment tax was 0%, GST may have increased the cost of movie tickets.

I Am Gen Y: GST for E-Commerce Businesses

Hey GG, I have recently started selling some goods through Amazon. Could you please help me with certain GST stuff?

Sure, Sanjay … shoot!

Well, to begin with, I think I do not have to charge GST on sale of goods because I have just started my business and have not crossed the threshold limit to obtain registration.

Well, Sanjay, while you may be right that your turnover has still not crossed the threshold limit and, hence, you do not have to charge GST, GST law has an exception for person selling goods through e-commerce operators like Amazon, Flipkart, Myntra, etc. (let's just call them ECOs henceforth). Irrespective of the value of turnover, every person selling goods through an e-commerce platform will have to obtain registration under GST, and charge GST from the buyers.

Further, every such ECO is also required to register, irrespective of the turnover.

Okay. But GG, all my payments are routed through Amazon. Amazon receives the payment on my behalf and then passes on the same to me. What will happen in such a case?

Well, you would still have to be registered under GST. However, where payments are received through an ECO, it is the duty of such an ECO to collect TCS on the payment received on your behalf and pay the net balance amount (net of TCS) to you.

TCS? What is that?

TCS is Tax Collected at Source. It is tax collected by the operator on payments received by it on behalf of the supplier providing goods or services through its e-commerce platform. TCS provisions are applicable for both supplier of goods and services. For example: You sell goods worth ₹100 to Mr X on Amazon. Mr X pays ₹100 for said goods. Amazon receives this amount on your behalf. Now, before remitting the said ₹100 to you, GST law provides for Amazon to collect TCS on the said amount. So, Amazon would collect TCS of ₹1 (1% of ₹100) and remit ₹99 to you (100 - 1).

Oh! So what is Amazon going to do with that Re. 1? And why should I not be paid the full amount for my goods?

Don't worry! Amazon would deposit Re.1 to the government within the specified time period and you can then set off the same amount against your final GST liability. The TCS collected is towards your GST liability. Therefore, at the month-end, when you deposit GST with the government, the amount of GST that you would have to deposit would be calculated as follows:

GST on sale of ₹100 = ₹18 (18% of ₹100)

TCS already collected = ₹1

Hence, total GST to be deposited = ₹17 (18–1)

And what about the goods returned by customers?

TCS is required to be collected only on net payments received, i.e. net of goods returned. For example: if you have made a total sale of ₹1,000 to Mr X, out of which Mr X returned goods worth ₹200, Amazon would receive ₹800 on your behalf. Therefore, TCS would be collected on ₹800 and not on ₹1,000.

You mentioned earlier that I can adjust the TCS collected by Amazon against my GST liability. How can I do that?

Oh, that's the beauty of the GSTN developed by the government. Everything under GST is inter-connected and such details get reflected automatically in a person's account. By this

I mean, when an ECO deposits the tax collected with the government, the tax so deposited gets reflected in the original registered seller's GST return form—GSTR-2A (on whose account such collection has been made). The seller can claim set-off while paying their GST liability.

Oh! You mean to say that when Amazon deposits the one-rupee-TCS collected from me with the government, Re. 1 would automatically be reflected in my GSTR-2A? And then I can take the credit of this ₹1 while paying my output GST liability on ₹100. Is that right?

You understood it perfectly well, my dear friend!

I was thinking of something else. You mentioned earlier that a person selling goods through an ECO does not have the benefit of a threshold limit to obtain registration. Does that mean that service providers providing services through an ECO like Ola, Uber, Oyo Rooms, etc., have the benefit of the threshold limit?

You are absolutely right, Sanjay! The mandatory registration is only for a person selling goods through ECO. Service providers enjoy the benefit of a threshold limit even while providing services through an ECO.

In case of the following services provided through the ECO, the liability to pay GST has been shifted to the ECO and, accordingly, the service provider is not required to obtain registration:

1. Transportation of passenger by taxis.
2. Accommodation services like hotels, inns, guest houses, camps, etc. (having a turnover of less than ₹20 lakh).
3. Housekeeping, plumbing, carpentry (having a turnover of less than ₹20 lakh).

In other words, if the total turnover of an entity supplying hotel, camp site, housekeeping services, etc. is more than ₹20 lakh in a year, then GST will be paid by that entity only, but ECO will deduct TCS @ 1%.

GG, could you please elaborate? I have friends who are in the business of plying taxis, running hotels and managing housekeeping, who are providing services through E-commerce platforms.

Okay, let me explain the details of each sector:

1. *Taxi Services*: If a person provides taxi services through say, an Ola or an Uber, he is not required to register under GST, irrespective of his turnover, and only the ECO (Ola or Uber) would be required to pay GST.
2. *Accommodation Services*: If a person is running a hotel where the booking is done through an ECO (say, Oyo Rooms) and the annual turnover is less than ₹20 lakh, then registration under GST will not be required, and GST will be paid by the said ECO. But, if the annual turnover is more than ₹20 lakh, then registration under GST would be required and, accordingly, GST will also have to be paid on the due dates.
3. *Housekeeping Services*: Same as accommodation services.
4. *Other Services*: In case of other service providers like restaurants operating through ECOs (say, Swiggy), if the turnover is less than ₹20 lakh, they are not required to register and pay GST. Even the ECO is not required to deduct TCS.

Also, just as in the case of goods, if services are supplied through an ECO, TCS of 1% shall be deducted by the ECO and the balance amount will be paid to the supplier. The TCS paid to the government by the ECO will be available as credit to the service provider.

Okay, thanks! By the way, GG, I also want to start selling books on Amazon. Since books are zero-tax goods, would all of the above provisions still apply?

It's a good question, Sanjay. Since you would be supplying both taxable and non-taxable goods, GST registration would be mandatory for you. However, If you had *only* sold exempt or non-taxable or zero-tax goods, you would have been exempted from taking registration. Also, TCS is collected only on the taxable value of goods sold. Since the sale of books is not taxable, TCS will not be collected. However, TCS *would* be collected on the payments received for sale of taxable goods.

May I please ask one last question?

Of course you may!

I have a friend who is running his own website and sells his own goods through it. Does he also become an ECO?

As per GST law, ECO is a person who owns, operates and manages a digital or electronic facility or platform that supplies goods or services over a digital or electronic network. Accordingly, your friend is also an ECO.

So, all the provisions we discussed above are applicable to him?

As per GST law, every ECO is mandatorily required to obtain registration. In other words, the threshold limit is not applicable, even for an ECO. However, TCS provisions will not be applicable to him, as TCS is applicable only when other sellers are selling through your e-commerce platform.

Okay, thank you so much GG, for your gyan on e-commerce!

Buying a House: How GST Impacts Real Estate Transactions

How are you doing, GG? I plan to put my money in real estate. Could you run me through some of the important points, from the perspective of GST, that I should consider before buying a house?

Real estate is one of the sectors that has been majorly impacted by GST. First, demonetisation and then, the introduction of GST—both impacted purchases and sales of realty and resulted in the industry plummeting to an all-time slowdown.

At the time of the introduction of GST, input tax credit was also extended to real estate industry on inputs used for construction of buildings. But at the same time, the rate of GST was kept at a higher level of 12%. However, on account of the availability of input tax credit, the cost of construction for developers was reduced, as the cascading effect of taxes was eliminated. The benefit of input tax credit is that, it lowers the price of the final product. Accordingly, developers should have passed on the benefit of input tax credit in the form of lower prices to home buyers.

However, many buyers complained that builders have not reduced the prices and have pocketed the tax credit benefits. In view of these complaints, and in order to benefit home buyers, the GST council—with effect from 1 April 2019—slashed GST rates from 12% to 5% on residential buildings. However, the input tax credit benefit was withdrawn. This way, the government ensured that the primary motive of the introduction of GST would not get defeated and instead, continue to benefit the end consumers by way of reduced prices of end products.

Some of the points that one can take care while buying real estate are illustrated in Table 14.1.

TABLE 14.1

Sl. No.	Scenarios	Treatment under GST
1.	Buying a ready-to-move-in property, both residential and commercial (where Completion Certificate, CC, has been obtained)	No GST is applicable on purchase of ready-to-move-in property (where CC has been obtained)

Sl. No.	Scenarios	Treatment under GST
2.	Buying an under construction* residential property **Under construction property means a property for which CC has not been issued by concerned authorities*	GST at the rate of 5% is applicable, with no benefit of input tax credit available to the builder
3.	Where agreement to buy a house has been entered into with the builder, prior to obtaining CC, but part payment for the house has been made after obtaining CC	If any amount (say ₹1 lakh) has been paid by the buyer prior to obtaining CC, GST would be applicable on full amount payable to the builder for purchase of house, including the amount paid subsequent to obtaining CC
4.	Registration of agreement to purchase the house with Stamp Duty authorities, subsequent to obtaining CC	If any amount is received prior to obtaining CC, GST would be applicable on full amount payable to the builder even though registration of agreement was made subsequent to obtaining CC
5.	Buying a property under affordable housing scheme* **Affordable housing means flats costing up to ₹45 lakh and measuring 60 sq. metres in metro cities and 90 sq. metres in non-metro cities*	GST at the rate of 1% is applicable, with no benefit of input tax credit available to the builder

»

Sl. No.	Scenarios	Treatment under GST
6.	Other charges by builder like, preferential location charges/floor raise charges/club house construction charges, etc.	These charges form part of the total price of the flat, and so GST treatment would be the same as it would be for sale of the flat
7.	Interest on delayed payment of demand raised by builder	GST is applicable at same rate as applicable to construction activity
8.	Stamp duty and property registration fee	Stamp duty and registration fee is not subsumed under GST and continues to be levied separately by the state governments, apart from GST
9.	Resale of property	Buying of property from secondary market does not attract GST
10.	Home loans:	
	Interest on home loans	GST is not applicable as interest paid on loans is kept out of the ambit of GST
	Loan processing fee or any other charges or fee for processing of loans	GST at the rate of 18% is applicable on such charges
	Prepayment of home loan	Any prepayment charges levied by the bank for early payment of loan will attract GST at the rate of 18%

Sl. No.	Scenarios	Treatment under GST
11.	Renting: Of residential property	No GST is applicable if the property is used for the purpose of residence
	Of commercial property	GST at the rate of 18% is applicable, if any property is rented for commercial purposes *Note: GST would be applicable only when the total value of all taxable services provided by a person crosses the threshold limit of ₹20 lakh*
12.	Maintenance charges by housing society	If monthly maintenance charge per flat is more than ₹7,500, then GST at the rate of 18% would be applicable on such maintenance charges. If it is less than ₹7,500, per flat, no GST is payable. However, if the total turnover of co-operative housing society (commonly called as Resident's Welfare Association) is less than ₹20 lakh, GST is not payable, irrespective of amount of monthly maintenance charges
	Interest for late payment of maintenance charges	GST at the rate of 18% is applicable, if GST was payable on maintenance charges.
	Charges by housing society towards sinking fund/repairs and maintenance fund/car parking charges	GST at the rate of 18% is applicable.

»

Sl. No.	Scenarios	Treatment under GST
13.	Buying or selling of land	GST is not applicable on sale of land
14.	Own land given by an individual to a contractor to build a house for residential purpose	Labour services provided by the contractor for construction of single residential unit (like bungalow or villa) is kept out of the ambit of GST However, GST on goods used for the construction of said single residential unit would be applicable
15.	Whether GST provisions are the same for residential and commercial property	No, on commercial property, normal GST rate of 12% is applicable with benefit of input tax credit. However, GST compliance procedures are the same for both.

Thanks, GG, for all the relevant information. GST does seem to have brought about some sort of transparency in the real estate industry.

Yes, that is true. Real estate is one sector in India where it is believed that the highest amount of black money is generated.The initial GST provision allowed input tax credit on all goods and services used for construction and this was intended to increase transparency and reduce tax evasion.

Also, now, the government requires builders to purchase minimum 80% of the total goods and services used for construction, with an invoice showing the payment of GST. If the builders fail to do so, they would be required to pay additional tax to the extent of purchase of goods and services without payment of GST. This way, the government believes that it has dealt with the menace of sale of goods without invoices and generation of black money.

I guess I can now finally decide about where to put my money in real estate.

Remember what we discussed. At this point, buying a ready-to-move-in-flat would be a better option than buying a property that is still being constructed, as GST would not be applicable on the purchase of a flat where CC has been obtained by the builder.

Yes, I will keep that in mind. Thank you.

Time to Buy a Car: How GST Has Affected the Prices of Automobiles

Hey GG, I am planning to buy a car. How has GST affected the price of cars?

GST has improved transparency in the amount of taxes that are levied to a great extent—especially in the case of automobiles. Earlier, a lot of taxes like excise duty, VAT, CST, auto cess, surcharges like National Calamity Contingent Duty (NCCD), octroi duty, entry tax, vehicle tax, etc. were levied at different stages of the consumer chain of the sale of automobiles. A lot of these taxes were not even visible to the end consumer and formed part of the cost of the autombile. With GST, most of these taxes are subsumed (except vehicle tax) and the consumer can see the actual amount of tax that he/she has to pay. There are no hidden tax costs and the consumer has become more aware of the taxation system in the country.

Most of the automobile companies introduced great discounts prior to the GST implementation, in order to make the most of the uncertainties around the GST rates on automobiles.

Under the GST regime, the only taxes that are levied on automobiles are CGST and SGST or IGST, and compensation cess.

Compensation cess? What is that?

Compensation Cess

Compensation cess is a levy charged by the government to compensate the states for the loss of revenue due to implementation of GST. Before GST, states levied a number of taxes on various transactions of goods or services like VAT, CST, entertainment tax, octroi duty, purchase tax, etc. to sustain itself from the tax revenue. Under the GST regime, states get revenue mainly from SGST levied on various transactions. Also, with the introduction of IGST in place of CST, tax collection for inter-state sales has shifted from manufacturing/originating state to the consumption states (since GST is a destination-based tax). This has led to a loss of revenue, mainly for states with a lot of manufacturing activity.

When the implementation of GST was being discussed, one of the major reasons for a lot of states to initially disagree was the loss of revenue occurring to them. To indemnify this loss, the Central government agreed to pay the states compensation for a period of five years (or pay for more years if the need so arose) from 1 July 2017.

Is compensation cess levied on supply of all goods and services?

No, it is levied only on the supply of the following goods or services:

1. Pan masala.
2. Tobacco, including tobacco products.
3. Coal.
4. Aerated waters.
5. Motor vehicles.
6. Any other supplies that the government may notify in the future.

And does every person supplying the above goods have to pay compensation cess?

Compensation cess has to be paid in the scenarios illustrated in Table 15.1.

TABLE 15.1

Scenarios	Whether Compensation Cess Is to Be Paid	Comments, If Any
Domestic Sale	Yes	Only for the products already mentioned above
Exports	No	If the exporter has paid cess on export of goods, then the cess would be refunded to him. Also, any cess paid on procurement of goods or services will also be refunded to the exporter, thus making export of goods zero rated from tax
Imports	Yes	Cess has to be paid at the time of payment of customs duty
Person Paying Tax under Composition Scheme	No	

So, this means that the cost of automobiles has increased because of compensation cess?

Compensation cess paid on procurement of goods or services to manufacture the final product can be set-off against the liability to pay compensation cess on the final product. This would ensure that tax on tax is avoided and only the value addition gets taxed. Hence, compensation cess would not *completely* form part of the cost of an automobile.

However, it is to be noted that compensation cess cannot be set-off against liability to pay GST on the final product.

Okay, so now, if I have to buy a car, then both GST and compensation cess will be levied, right?

Compensation cess on a few, small-category cars is not applicable. For other cars, yes, both GST and cess will be applicable.

Can you help me with the impact of GST on various types of automobiles vis-à-vis the old tax regime?

Sure. The graph illustrated in Figure 15.1 shows just that.

Impact of GST on Various Kinds of Automobiles

FIGURE 15.1

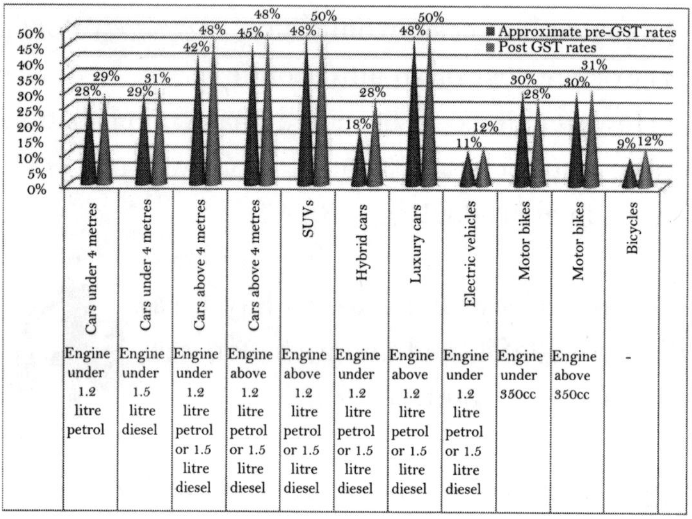

*Note: Pre-GST rates are a total of excise duty, auto cess and VAT. These are approximate rates and may vary according to each state and other levies like CST, road tax, etc., which may vary in each scenario. GST rates are indicative and are a total of GST and compensation cess.

As can be seen, there is a marginal increase in the tax rate under GST regime, but in the long run, GST would have benefits for this industry. Elimination of cascading effect of taxes and availability of credit at every stage would reduce the overall cost of the product. Also, credit availability of IGST would be a big advantage since it would reduce the tax cost (in the earlier regime, credit of CST was not available, thus forming part of the final product). All this is likely to lead to reduction of overall tax cost in the automobile supply chain. This optimisation of the tax cost could possibly benefit the end consumer by way of a likely reduction in automobile prices in the future.

Okay, judging from that analysis, I am now wondering whether I should buy an old used car instead of a new car. Would GST still be applicable on a second-hand car?

Impact of GST on Purchase and Sale of Second-Hand Cars

Prior to GST, the applicability of taxes on second-hand cars varied from state to state.

While some states did not charge VAT on sale of second-hand cars, other states charged an approximate of 12.5% to 15% of VAT on the sale value of second-hand cars by registered dealers. Some states like Maharashtra had introduced a composition system, where VAT at 15% was applicable on the sale value of second-hand cars.

Tax treatment under GST, on purchase of second-hand cars, is as follows:

1. *Purchase of a Second-Hand Car from a Friend or Relative or Any Other Individual:* GST is applicable on the supply of goods or services, if the supply is in the course or furtherance of business. In this case, neither the seller nor the buyer are selling or purchasing the car in the course of business, hence, no GST is applicable.
2. *Purchase of a Second-Hand Car from an Unregistered Second-Hand Dealer:* In this case, the second-hand dealer, from whom you buy the old car, buys or sells old cars in the course of or furtherance of his/her business. However, since he/she is not registered under GST (possibly because he/she has not reached the threshold limit of ₹40 lakh/₹20 lakh, as the case maybe), no GST would be applicable even in this case.

3. *Purchase from a Registered Second-Hand Dealer:* If you buy a used car from a dealer registered under GST, then tax would be applicable on the purchase of such a second-hand car. The government, in this case, has, however, provided some relaxation. In case of the purchase of used cars, GST is applicable only on the margin of the sale of car, i.e. the registered dealer would charge GST on the value shown below:

Margin = Sale price of old car – Purchase price of the old car.

If, in the above case, margin is zero or negative, then no GST would be applicable on the transaction.

GST on such a margin would be applicable at the rates prescribed by the government.

Normally, GST is charged on the transaction value of sale of goods. This relaxation is provided by the government for used cars to avoid double taxation, as tax credit is not available to the original consumer at the time of purchase of new car and is also not available to the registered second-hand dealer on the purchase of used car from the original consumer. The goods have once borne the incidence of tax and have again re-entered the economic supply chain. Hence, only value addition gets taxed in this case.

The above benefit of margin scheme shall be available only if the following conditions are satisfied:

(a) The old goods should be re-sold by the registered dealer as they are, or after minor processing which does not change the nature of the goods.

(b) No input tax credit should be availed on the purchase of second-hand goods by the registered dealer.

Instead of buying a secondhand car, what if I exchanged my old car for the new one in an exchange offer? What would the GST impact be, in such a case?

In an exchange offer, GST is charged on the sale value of the new car, irrespective of said offer. For example, if the value of a new car is ₹5 lakh, but the purchaser in an exchange offer pays only ₹4 lakh, GST would be levied on ₹5 lakh.

Okay. And what if I just want to sell my old car, without buying a new one? Would GST be levied even then?

As mentioned earlier, GST is levied on any supply of goods and services made in the course or furtherance of business. Sale of old car by an individual to any person does not mean it is supplied in the course or furtherance of business. Therefore, no GST would be levied on the sale of old car by an individual to any person.

Okay, one final question, GG. If I take a loan to finance my car, would GST be applicable? Also, would interest paid to service the loan attract GST?

Impact of GST on Loan Taken to Purchase a Car

GST is levied on the supply of goods or services. Since the loan amount is neither goods nor services, GST is not applicable.

Also, the government has specifically kept interest paid by a person on loan *out* of the ambit of GST. However, any processing fee or administrative charges paid to process the loan is taxable under GST.

Taxpayer-Friendly Measures

Hi GG! Can you tell me if the government has specifically undertaken any taxpayer-friendly measures which would benefit the ultimate consumer or, in general, a person paying GST?

GST was introduced to benefit the industry and the consumers. The subsuming of multiple taxes into one and the availability of input tax credit at every stage in the consumer chain are the highlights of the GST regime, benefiting industry, consumers and the government alike.

Apart from that, the government has been very responsive and prompt in making constant changes in law where the implementation of law has been difficult. For instance, when GST was launched, its portal had a lot of technical issues. But the government improvised constantly to make it more taxpayer-friendly. The government also heard the pleas of industry and consumers and changed the tax rates on a lot of products, so as to reduce the tax burden.

Apart from these, the two major taxpayer-friendly measures that the government undertook are:

1. Constituting the National Anti-Profiteering Authority (NAPA), for the benefit of end consumers.
2. Constituting Authority for Advance Ruling (AAR), for the benefit of business houses.

Can we discuss these two in detail?

Sure, let us look at them, one at a time.

National Anti-Profiteering Authority

NAPA was constituted to protect the consumers from arbitrary increases in the prices of goods or services in the name of GST. Reduction in tax rate because of GST or availability of input tax credit at every stage in the consumer chain should result in reduction in prices of most goods and services. One of the purposes of the introduction of GST was to benefit the end consumer from the burden of innumerable taxes; hence, the benefit of reduced tax rate or availability of input tax credit should reach consumers by way of reduced prices.

NAPA's main objective is to ensure that if the prices of goods or services have reduced due to GST, the same must reach the consumers and not be pocketed by business houses—because, while profit is fine, undue profiteering at the expense of the lay person must not be allowed.

This seems very interesting—especially from the point of view of a consumer like me. We have struggled a lot, especially in the initial days of GST, when the price of almost everything was inflated.

Don't you think there should be a forum where consumers can file a complaint against such businesses if they do not pass on the benefit of GST to us, rather than waiting for the government to catch hold of them?

Of course there is!

An aggrieved consumer can file a complaint of profiteering through the following ways:

1. File an online complaint at www.naa.gov.in.
2. Send an email to secretary.naa@gov.in or sc.antiprofiteering@gov.in.
3. Send a post to:

(a) National Anti-Profiteering Authority, 6th floor, Tower One, Jeevan Bharti, Connaught Place, New Delhi – 110001.

(b) Standing Committee, Directorate General of Anti-Profiteering, 2nd floor, Bhai Veer Singh Sahitya Sadan, Bhai Veer Singh Marg, Gole Market, New Delhi – 110001.

4. Call helpline number: 011–21400643 (meant for resolving queries related to registering of complaints and providing information regarding anti-profiteering).

What does NAPA do once it receives a complaint of profiteering against a business?

NAPA's actions can be viewed in Figure 16.1

FIGURE 16.1

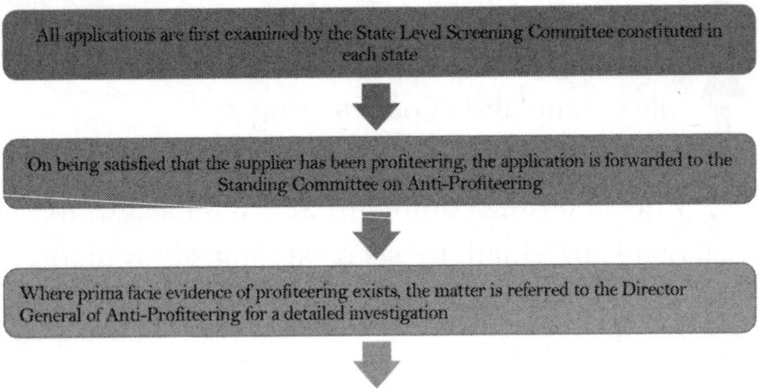

The Director General of Anti-Profiteering will conduct a detailed investigation by issuing notices and conducting hearings with concerned parties to gather further information. It can also seek the opinion of any other agency or statutory authority to conclude its proceedings

After receiving the report from the Director General, NAPA will pass its order. If the person is found guilty of profiteering, NAPA may order:
- Reduction in price of product
- To compensate the consumer with an amount that should have been passed as benefit to him/her (along with interest)
- Payment of penalty for engaging in profiteering
- Cancellation of GST registration

Wow! But the cancellation of a GST registration might be a bit draconian, don't you think?

That would be NAPA's last resort. Moreover, these provisions serve as a deterrent for companies.

It is definitely very helpful for consumers. But sometimes the consumers may, because of lack of knowledge, unnecessarily file a complaint against a business and harass them.

That is true. But there have been many cases reported in the past where businesses have been cleared of profiteering charges because, after detailed investigation, it was found that

they did not engage in profiteering as complained of by consumers. A few examples that were reported in dailies, were of a car dealer in Ahmedabad and another car dealer in Bareily—both of whom were exonerated from charges of profiteering filed by consumers who had bought cars from them. These instances prove that unwarranted harassments will not be entertained by the government and so, businesses which honestly conduct their business need not worry.

Okay, and till date, have there been cases where NAPA ruled in favour of the consumer?

Yes. It was again reported in the dailies that a big fast-food chain company was reportedly guilty of not passing the benefit of reduced tax rate to consumers when GST rate was reduced from 18% to 5% on restaurant services. Said company was ordered to refund the amount which should have been the price reduction, along with interest at the rate of 18% to the applicant filing the complaint.

Apart from this, the government has also voluntarily sent a lot of notices to MNCs which they suspected of not having passed on the benefit of GST to consumers, and final orders have been passed after proper investigation.

Oh, yes! I also recall some of these instances. Some industries were not passing on the benefit of input tax credit to consumers by way of reduced prices. In response to this, the government heeded the pleas of consumers and denied the benefit of input tax credit to these industries and reduced the rate of GST, so that the end consumers benefit from it in the form of reduced prices. *(These can be seen in Table 16.1.)*

TABLE 16.1

Industry	Old GST Rate (With Benefit of ITC)	New GST Rate (Without the Benefit of ITC)
Restaurant	18%	5%
Purchase of under-Construction Property	12%	5%
Purchase of under-Construction Property (under affordable housing scheme)	8%	1%

That's right. There have also been some companies who have passed on the benefit of GST to consumers and have proudly announced the same. *(This can be seen in Figure 16.2)*

FIGURE 16.2

With NAPA around, I guess we can stop worrying about unnecessary price hikes.

NAPA was initially constituted for only two years, as the government felt that the industry would settle into GST in two years' time and that prices of the products would also stabilise by then. It has now decided to extend NAPA's tenure for another two years, after analysing the current scenario.

Let us now discuss the second taxpayer-friendly measure that the government has taken.

Sure!

Authority for Advance Ruling

Any corporation or individual confused about the tax treatment of an activity proposed to be undertaken or being undertaken by them can seek a solution at Authority for Advance Ruling (AAR) in order to resolve tax ambiguity for that transaction. The applicant to AAR can achieve clarity about the tax liability it would have to incur on a particular activity undertaken or to be undertaken by it.

The applicant can plan their activities from the perspective of GST well in advance and save time and money in any potential tax litigation that may happen in future. Advance ruling is an inexpensive and simple procedure which provides certainty and transparency to the taxpayer and even to the jurisdictional revenue authority, as advance ruling is binding on both the applicant and the jurisdictional revenue authority.

Some of the important aspects of AAR can be seen in Figure 16.3.

FIGURE 16.3

Matters or Questions Regarding Which Advance Ruling Can Be Sought

- Classification of goods or services
- Applicability of a notification issued under GST Act
- Determination of time and value of supply of goods or services
- Availability of input tax credit
- Determination of liability to pay GST on supply of goods or services
- Whether applicant is required to be registered under GST

Ruling by AAR

- The ruling by AAR is binding on both the applicant and jurisdictional tax authorities. Tax authorities cannot take a different tax position in future which is different from the ruling of AAR, thus avoiding any tax litigation
- Ruling by AAR is applicable ONLY on the applicant. It is not binding on any other taxpayer with the same or a similar transaction. The other taxpayer can, however, use the ruling as a persuasive value for taxability of his own transaction
- Advance ruling shall be binding as long as the transaction continues and as long as there is no change in law, facts or circumstances of the case
- If the applicant is aggrieved with the ruling of AAR, they can file an appeal with Appellate Authority for Advance Ruling (AAAR)
- No further appeal can be filed against the order of AAAR. Order of AAAR is final and binding on the applicant and the jurisdictional tax authorities. However, a writ can be filed in high court or Supreme Court

Procedure for Obtaining Advance Ruling

- Application to AAR can be made in Form GST ARA-01 and can be filed on the GSTN portal or manually at the tax office. The application filed should be accompanied with the prescribed fee
- AAR will not admit the application if the same transaction for which AAR is sought is pending for decision in any other proceeding of the applicant or the verdict on the same transaction has been given in any earlier case of the applicant
- Once AAR recieves the application, it shall send a copy of the application to the jurisdictional tax officer. After examining all the records placed before it and hearing the applicant, AAR will pass its ruling within 90 days of receipt of application
- If the applicant or the jurisdictional tax officer is aggrieved by the order of AAR, they can file an appeal to AAAR within 30 days from the order of AAR
- AAAR, after examining the facts of the case and giving parties an opprtunity to be heard, shall pass its order within 90 days from the receipt of appeal
- If members of AAAR differ on any point referred to in appeal, then no advance ruling will be given on that matter

An advance ruling seems like a good time-saving tool for business houses. Industries ought to be very happy with this measure.

Yes. People do take advantage of advance ruling sometimes, but even the measure itself has some shortcomings.

What kind of shortcomings?

Taxpayers have expressed unhappiness with the functioning of AAR/ AAAR for the following reasons:

1. AAR comprises two members: one, a CGST member and the other, an SGST member—both of whom are appointed by Central and state governments respectively. It does not have any judicial member, separate from a tax authority. This has increased the chances of a ruling being in favour of revenue and may not be very beneficial for the applicant.
2. The elected members of AAR are junior-level officers (like joint commissioners). In the service tax regime, AAR had senior members, like retired Supreme Court judges and other members who were at the level of chief commissioners. This has also affected the quality of rulings given by AAR.
3. A pro-revenue ruling by any state AAR encourages other state AARs to issue similar ruling in similar transactions which may not be the right verdict and be harsh on the taxpayer.
4. Each state has its own AAR and AAAR. This has led to a situation of different tax positions taken by different AARs, in cases with similar fact patterns. Even though an advance ruling is applicable only to the applicant, yet another taxpayer can use the ruling as a persuasive value for their own

> transactions. But with different tax opinions offered by different AARs in different states, a taxpayer may become confused about their business decisions. However, Budget 2019 proposed to create a national AAR to decide cases of companies that have a presence in more than one state but have different rulings on the same issue by different state AARs.

Hence, AAR's track record thus far has not been exceptional.

How Is the Government Engaging with the People?

GST has been the biggest tax reform in the history of India. It completely overhauled the existing indirect tax regime of India. In fact, both industry and taxpayers struggled a lot in the initial days of its implementation—and many still find it difficult to understand. I wish the government could do something about it to educate and guide people so that they may easily figure out GST law.

The government did realise the struggles of people and tried to ease taxpayers into the GST regime.

Keeping in mind all nature of technological advancements, the government tried to provide a lot of help through various means. Technology is easily accessible to people nowadays and is, in fact, the most preferred way of operating for a lot of people. The methods that the government employed can be seen in Figure 17.1.

FIGURE 17.1

YouTube Channel ('GST_INDIA')	• Regularly uploads videos to provide information on GST to consumers • Videos are aimed to create awareness amongst consumers and industry, and educate them about the latest major amendments in GST • #GG_Review: The quality and the content of videos is good
Official Twitter Handles ('@askGST_GoI' and '@askGSTech')	• '@askGST_GoI' was introduced in 2017 in order to give prompt responses to taxpayers regarding queries asked on Twitter. The replies were prompt and this handle was a success. However, from August 2018, the government declared that it would no longer reply to the queries on this handle. The initital struggle was over and so this instant query redressal forum was stopped. The government felt that the queries that taxpayers now have can wait and don't need an immediate response • @askGSTech was started to handle GSTN/GST IT-related queries. Regular updates and changes in the online GST portal are announced here. It helps to keep abreast with any changes in GST compliance procedures

CBEC Mitra Helpdesk	• It is a helpdesk which serves as a one-stop shop for all GST-related queries or complaints for both taxpayers as well as departmental officers
	• Three modes of complaints can be registered on this helpdesk, viz.:
	  • Calling the toll free no: 1800 1200 232 (24*7 helpdesk)
	  • Sending an email at: cbecmitra.helpdesk@icegate.gov.in
	  • Web-ticketing at https://cbec-gst.gov.in/help.html > Self Service
	• Status of any query/complaint can be tracked through SMS by quoting the acknowledgment number using the toll-free SMS service
	• To continously improve its services, the government regularly takes feedback from its users about the quality of service provided to them

GSTN-related Issues	• For any query arising while working on the GST portal or GSTN, the consumer can directly raise a ticket on that website itself
	• Helps the taxpayer or other stakeholder to lodge a complaint directly, without having to send emails to helpdesk, which helps in quick redressal of griveance
	• Complaint can be reported at:
	  • https://www.gst.gov.in/ > Help; or
	  • https://selfservice.gstsystem.in/

GST App ('CBEC GST')	• The government even created an app for use on mobile phones
	• It contains the GST Act, Rules, Notifications, Circulars, FAQs, GST rates of products and services, helpdesk, etc.
	• #GG_Review
	  • The biggest drawback of the app is that, it is not updated and does not contain latest amendments in the GST law
	  • A lot of notifications and circulars which are in 'Pdf' format do not open on the mobile
	  • The layout of the app is also not very good

The Official CBIC Website (http://www.cbic.gov.in)	• This official website contains everything related to indirect taxes • It contains everything about GST: GST Act, Rules, Notifications, Circulars, FAQs, GST rates of products and services, indsutry-wise flyers, sectoral FAQs, topic-wise FAQs, write-ups on all important topics of GST, all latest amendments, GST helpdesk, etc. • #GG_Review serves as a one-stop destination for all information on GST rules and regulations. It is regularly updated and so one cannot miss out on latest amendments
Weekly Update Presentation	• CBIC website > GST > GST Background material > NACIN GST weekly update • This powerpoint presentation is made by the government and covers all important amendments that have been made in GST law in the past week • #GG_Review is in an easy and brief format, which makes it simple to keep abreast with latest amendments
GST Awareness Campaign - *Manthan* (https://gstawareness.cbec.gov.in/)	• This campaign was launched by the government to ensure preparedness of the taxpayers for implementation of GST from 1 July 2017 • GST awareness programmes like training workshops, seminars, town hall meetings, trade interactions, etc. were held across the country • More than 10,000 such events were held nation-wide • Such events are not held any more

About the Author

Apeksha Solanki is a qualified chartered accountant and has a rich experience of working with the Big 4 accounting firms in the fields of both direct and indirect taxes.

Apeksha has actively taken part in seminars and study circles of the Institute of Chartered Accountants of India. Over the last couple of years, she has focussed on writing fiction, including book reviews. She has also been an active participant in discussion groups where fresh publications by various authors are discussed.

Her love for the written word began with the Harry Potter series. She is a passionate dancer and loves to travel, and wishes that one day she could make an impact on the society.

For the last seven years, Apeksha has left her nomadic life with her parents and now lives in Delhi with her workaholic husband, a trouble-making infant and her father-in-law.

SBD
RN. 18668
Bloomsbury
20/8/20